HELPING
A LOVED ONE LIVE
SMOKE-FREE

HELPING
A LOVED ONE LIVE
SMOKE-FREE

What Works, What Won't, *and Why*

Barbara White Melin

HAZELDEN®

Hazelden
Center City, Minnesota 55012-0176

1-800-328-0094
1-651-213-4590 (Fax)
www.hazelden.org

ISBN: 1-56838-787-3

06 05 04 03 02   6 5 4 3 2 1

Cover design by David Spohn
Interior design by Rachel Holscher
Typesetting by Stanton Publication Services, Inc.

To my grandfathers,
Edward S. Bradley and Albert T. White,
In loving memory

CONTENTS

ᔧ Acknowledgments ᔩ

I wish to express grateful acknowledgment to my agent, Jeanne K. Hanson, for taking a chance on a new idea from an unknown writer and persisting until she found the right match; to my editor, Karen Chernyaev, for her excellent judgment and painstaking attention to detail in fine-tuning my manuscript through numerous revisions; to my family, especially my parents, Albert and Dolores White, and my son, Eric Melin, for their love and encouragement during all my attempts to quit smoking; and last but not least, to the volunteers and staff of the American Cancer Society, for their tireless dedication to the mission of reducing unnecessary suffering and death caused by tobacco.

✐ Part I ✑

◎ Introduction ◎

You've tried everything: Begging, pleading, bribery, tears, threats, maybe even trickery. You've cited statistics, referred to the warnings on the sides of cigarette packages, and quoted the U.S. Surgeon General until you're blue in the face. It's the most helpless feeling in the world, watching the life of someone you care about go up in smoke. It's like standing on the edge of a cliff and knowing a friend or loved one is about to fall—and not being able to do a single thing to stop it.

Maybe the smoker you care about has seriously tried to quit. Perhaps he keeps promising to quit. In all likelihood, he really wants to quit, but so far he hasn't. And you're worried sick.

There are good reasons for you to worry. Tobacco kills 1,100 people in the United States every day. That's almost one person per minute. Between 1998 and 2025, tobacco is projected to kill five hundred million people worldwide. That's a *Titanic* every forty-three minutes. It's a Vietnam War every day. According to former Surgeon General C. Everett Koop, if we were to build a memorial like the Vietnam Wall for these victims, it would stretch across seven states.[1]

Who wouldn't be frightened for someone they cared about who ran this kind of risk? It's like knowing that a loved one lived in a war zone and was deliberately running around outdoors in a hail of gunfire. What makes it worse is knowing that it's all so *unnecessary!* Smoking is a voluntary activity, isn't it? If you've never smoked, it's probably hard to understand why, in light of all the evidence, anyone would continue to smoke. Unless they've been living on Mars for the past few decades, smokers *know* how bad smoking is for them. Why don't they quit? Why don't they wise up? Why don't they take charge of their lives?

The reason many smokers can't quit is because they're addicted. *Addiction* may be defined as an uncontrollable appetite, an obsessive, chemically induced craving. The addictive element in tobacco—nicotine—has been recognized as harder to conquer than heroin or cocaine. Addiction has a way of forcing smokers to deny the evidence. Addicts can be absolute geniuses at denial. When they run out of denials, they become gamblers, betting against the odds that the dangers of smoking will pass them by. And when the odds catch up with them, their addiction can even overwhelm the most powerful human instinct of all—the instinct for survival.

Library and bookstore shelves are crammed with volumes on alcohol addiction. There are many books on cocaine, heroin, marijuana, stimulants, sedatives, and a host of prescription drugs. But addictions to these substances kill only a fraction of the number of people who die of tobacco-related diseases. Occasionally, books that focus on other addictions mention tobacco in passing, but usually it's only an afterthought. Nicotine addiction is more respectable than cocaine or alcohol addiction. After all, cigarettes and chew are products that are not only legal but, until recently, socially acceptable. It's only tobacco. It's not as if smokers were addicted to a really "dangerous" drug.

Granted, there are plenty of books about smoking. But smokers, in their denial, often ignore attempts to help them. And books aimed at smokers are becoming fewer in number. Even the nonprofit agencies that have traditionally reached out a helping hand to smokers are now placing their emphasis elsewhere. In all fairness, these agencies really have no choice. The dismal failure rates of many stop-smoking programs have forced these agencies to focus their limited resources in areas where they have better odds for success. This is unfortunate. What it means is that there are nearly fifty million people in the United States alone who are being written off as unsalvageable. Except, of course, by those who care for them.

There is no "Nic-Anon" for the parents, spouses, and friends of nicotine addicts. As for advice books aimed at those who watch helplessly as friends and loved ones puff their lives away, virtually none are to be found. These innocent bystanders have been forced to wait, worry, hope, and pray that someday the smokers they care about will find the strength or willpower or whatever it takes finally to quit.

This book is intended to fill that gap. The following pages include scientifically proven tobacco cessation treatments and communication techniques designed to motivate and inspire. This book describes knowledge I've acquired through my experience as a stop-smoking counselor and facilitator trainer. It also describes my experience as a former smoker who failed to quit nearly a dozen times before trial and error, along with determination and hard-won wisdom, led ultimately to success.

One thing experience has taught me is that smokers and chewers (let's not forget that chewing tobacco is still tobacco—and every bit as deadly) are just like other addicts. They need support from family and friends to overcome their addiction. But chances are you've been going about it the wrong way. Chances are you've been nagging, pleading, using bribery, tears, and threats, maybe even participating in their denial. Not only do these tactics fail to convince smokers to quit, but also, in many cases, they actually increase the desire to keep smoking.

There is hope. There are ways you can help. But before you can provide really effective assistance, you need to understand why people smoke and why it's so hard to quit. You should know something about the social conventions surrounding tobacco and the ways these conventions promote addiction. Finally, you will learn methods that can make a difference to smokers and hopefully help them break the addiction that's not only controlling their lives but also may eventually take their lives.

First, let me share my story.

◈ Chapter One ◈

MY STORY
I Was a Stop-Smoking School Dropout

When I was a child, I never thought I'd start smoking. I was a "good" kid. While I was growing up in the 1960s, it seemed to me that the only kids who smoked were "bad" kids, rebels with or without a cause. I was no rebel. I made good grades, I obeyed my parents, and I lived according to the rules of society. One of those rules was that kids, especially "good" kids, didn't smoke. Smoking was an adult habit. It was not something I ever saw myself taking up.

My mother hated smoking. She admitted having tried a cigarette once as a teenager but found it so obnoxious, she never tried it again. My father hated smoking, too. He had good reason to hate it. His own father died of emphysema when I was just five years old. Like most emphysema sufferers, my grandfather had been a heavy smoker, and his death was slow and miserable. But my dad's hatred of tobacco was equivocal, because he was a smoker himself. He had been an athlete in high school and never touched tobacco until he went away to basic training at Lackland Air Force Base in San Antonio, Texas, in the early 1950s. He used to carry chocolate bars to munch during breaks while other recruits smoked cigarettes. But chocolate doesn't do well in San Antonio in summer, and finally he switched to cigarettes to save his uniform pockets.

My dad always worried about smoking. He switched from cigarettes to a pipe before I was born and tried to give that up several times during my childhood. But inevitably the nicotine fits drove him back to it. I still remember how awful it was to drive anywhere in the winter with my dad because his pipe smoke always nauseated us in the closed car. We used to complain about being carsick, not realizing it was poisons in the pipe smoke that caused our symptoms. But in those days it was not considered irresponsible for adults to smoke around children, and smoking itself was regarded as a bad habit rather than a dangerous addiction. All the same, I hated smoking and vowed never to put my own children through the torment of being trapped in a closed, smoky car in the winter.

My father's military career forced us to move around a lot. This was tough on our family, but as Dad used to quip, "If the air force wanted you to have a family, they'd have issued you one." My parents did their best to create a secure family environment, but I grew up with feelings of rootlessness and insecurity. As a young child I was very shy, never speaking unless spoken to and only speaking then in a quiet, timid voice. In those days there were, and probably still are, adults who regarded this kind of reserve as a challenge. I have a stark memory of my first-grade teacher, who became irritated by my perpetually downcast eyes and barely audible voice. In an effort to cure me, she forced me to run around the classroom shouting "Hello!" loud enough for everyone to hear. I remember crying as I galloped past my tittering classmates and tried desperately to yell loud enough to satisfy the teacher who kept calling, "Louder, Barbara! Louder! We still can't hear you!" My sense of shame was such that I didn't mention this incident to anyone until I reached adulthood.

In time, I managed to overcome my bashfulness. Eventually, I became quite outspoken, but my natural introversion always reasserted itself whenever I was presented with a new situation. The air force obliged me by providing plenty of those. By the time I graduated from high school, I had been enrolled at no fewer than ten different schools. With so much practice, it should have grown easier, but every time we moved I suffered the agony of saying good-bye to old friends and struggling to make new ones. It will come as no surprise to any child psychologist that I grew up eager to please, as did my younger siblings, an attitude that leaves some kids vulnerable to the wrong kind of influences.

My younger sister was only eleven years old when she tried her first cigarette. It was offered to her by a new friend at an air force base in San Antonio (ironically, the same place my father had started smoking), where we had recently moved. In an effort to be sociable, she accepted, and by the time she was thirteen, she was a regular smoker. Then, as now, kids who smoked often experimented with other drugs. For my sister, tobacco was an initiation into a dangerous world. My younger brother, though a gifted athlete, started smoking at thirteen. Like my sister, this led him to try other drugs as well.

I was luckier than my brother and sister in that I linked up with an academically inclined crowd whose influence kept me on the straight and narrow through the early part of high school. I had tried smoking in junior high but didn't care for it and looked upon the antics of my younger siblings with disdain. My parents had meanwhile learned that my sister was smoking. My mother was especially distressed by this discovery, as she had recently learned that her father had emphysema. Having gone through it all years before with my paternal grandfather, my parents knew what lay ahead and could not understand how my sister could so easily ignore the evidence and care so little for her own future. But my sister was less concerned about the future than about fitting in with her friends. Besides, she was already addicted.

My father was transferred to a base in Colorado between my junior and senior years of high school. Every move we'd made had been tough, but this one was shattering. Not only was I leaving behind the best friends I'd ever had, but I was facing a definite time crunch in terms of creating a new social circle. I had only a year to fit into a new environment before graduation scattered everyone to the high winds, and by this time the inevitable cliques had pretty well solidified at the new school. Desperate to find a niche, I found one in the school's theatrical department. I had performed in a few plays in San Antonio, finding relief from adolescent self-consciousness behind various roles. But at my new school, the student actors imitated their Hollywood counterparts by smoking, drinking, and using drugs. Though I still shied away from alcohol and other drugs, I started smoking backstage with my fellow actors, occasionally joining them during breaks at the student smoking area, recently designated as part of a new open school policy. This also created an acceptance with my brother and sister, who had always regarded me as hopelessly square. At first, I nearly collapsed a lung every time I inhaled, but with practice I managed to perfect my technique. By the time I graduated from high school in 1974, I was smoking every day.

I didn't think I was doing anything all that terrible. After all, it was only tobacco. It wasn't as if I was smoking pot or dropping acid or doing anything really dangerous. My attitude toward tobacco had been shaped by movie and advertising portrayals of smoking as glamorous and a badge of independence. This was especially true of advertising aimed at young women. Though television ads for tobacco were officially banned in 1971, I still recall the tune and lyrics of the catchy Virginia Slims jingle, and the independent attitude those ads portrayed. To a young girl with years of pent-up resentment toward a paternalistic military culture, this was an image that appealed to me. My self-esteem, never high, was enhanced by the sophistication I thought cigarettes gave me. In addition, I'd always been a little on the pudgy side, and the pencil-thin models in all the cigarette ads, along with brand names like Virginia *Slims,* implied that cigarettes could help control my weight. Not coincidentally, the first cigarettes I smoked were Virginia Slims.

An even more seductive lure was the discovery that smoking helped relieve some of my darker moods. Even as a very young child, I recall experiencing unusually deep feelings of depression that my vagabond upbringing and poor self-image had exacerbated. Little was known then about clinical depression, and depression in children was almost unheard-of. All I knew was that when I smoked, I felt a lifting of my spirits. So between physiology, sociology, psychology, and advertising, I, too, became addicted.

When I started smoking, I honestly did not see myself as a smoker when I got older. Like most teenagers, I thought I could quit when I was old—say, twenty-five or so. By the time I was nineteen, I was already tired of it. I was sick of the smell, the expense, the sore throats, the cough, the red eyes, and the hassle of always having to carry cigarettes and matches around. So I decided to quit, thinking it would be a snap. After all, I had been smoking for only three years. But I was stunned at the way I felt when I tried to quit for the first time. I was light-headed, jittery, and overwhelmed by stark feelings of abject hopelessness. I worked then as a secretary in an office where smoking was the norm rather than the exception. I smoked during breaks, I kept a cigarette burning while I answered the phone or typed, and I enjoyed having a smoke during lunch with my buddies from the office. The man I was dating smoked, all my friends smoked, and after just one day without cigarettes, it was as easy to light up again as sliding down a greased pole.

There were things I liked about smoking, but there were a lot more I didn't like, and I was still determined to quit. To celebrate my twenty-first birthday, I tried again. By this time I was married. My husband also smoked, and I convinced him to quit with me. He lasted longer than I did. He stayed away from cigarettes for a whole week. I survived only a weekend, and it was so traumatic that I didn't try again for two more years. By then I was pregnant. And I was desperate to quit.

I did try. I threw my cigarettes away as soon as I began to suspect I might be pregnant. But after just two weeks, I started passing blood clots and experiencing painful cramps. I later learned that I'd had a miscarriage, and the resulting depression led me back to cigarettes. I don't know whether my smoking had anything to do with that miscarriage or not, and frankly I don't want to know. What I do know is that just three months later, I was pregnant again. And I was still smoking.

I tried switching to a low-nicotine brand and tapered down to half a pack a day, thinking I could quit more easily that way. I actually did quit in my fourth month. Though I suffered the usual jitters and anxiety attacks, I was determined to see it through for the sake of my unborn child. Then disaster struck. Within days of discarding my cigarettes, my maternal grandfather lost his long, desperate battle with emphysema.

I adored my grandfather, and his death was appalling. Emphysema is a slow suffocation that is horrible to watch. I visited my grandfather in the hospital two days before he died. My pregnancy was just beginning to show, and I knew how much he had been looking forward to seeing his great-grandchild. Through the haze of drugs and pain, he recognized me and tried to say something, but he lacked the breath to get it out. All I could see was the agonized look in his eyes as I ran, sobbing, into the hall. I waited until I had composed myself, then marched down to the waiting room where I remembered seeing a cigarette vending machine. I told myself I couldn't cope with the stress, but buying that pack of cigarettes still strikes me as the craziest thing I've ever done.

I continued to smoke through the remainder of my pregnancy but stayed with low-nicotine brands and tried to cut back to just five or six cigarettes a day. I smoked one on the way to the hospital. I smoked another halfway through an incredibly difficult twenty-hour labor that culminated in a seven-pound baby boy. But my new son cried continuously for the first three or four days of his life. He wouldn't nurse, wouldn't sleep, and couldn't be comforted. It wasn't until fifteen years later, when scientific evidence about the symptoms displayed by newborn babies whose mothers smoked during pregnancy was published, that I understood what I had done. My baby's symptoms were like those of crack babies in the first days after their birth. My son had been suffering from drug withdrawal because of the nicotine that had passed into his tiny body from mine. Today, more than twenty years later, this recollection makes me shudder. My son is now a healthy, handsome, intelligent young man, but I am still overcome with guilt when I think of the way his life began.

Soon after my son was born, my father succeeded in giving up tobacco, which he celebrated by turning into a zealot. Every smoker alive knows the type: The ex-smokers who "get religion" and preach about the evil of tobacco until their presence becomes an irritant. My younger sister now lived halfway across the country, but my brother and I both lived near our parents, and together we bore the brunt of what we regarded as our father's obsession. I have no doubt that he was motivated by love and concern, but his constant criticism only increased my desire to smoke. My father and I fought many battles over my smoking. His emphasis was always on the health risks, though he himself had been oblivious to those risks all the years he smoked.

Oddly enough, as much as I wanted to stop smoking, the health risks never really entered into it for me. Like most addicts, I was in total denial, or what author Herman Wouk described in *War and Remembrance* as "the will not to believe." A convict on the way to the gallows, a patient dying of cancer, a sailor on a ship going down to the briny deep often fails to accept the truth of her own mortality. Naturally, I was aware of the health risks of smoking, but diseases such as emphysema and lung cancer were too terrible to contemplate and way too far into the future to seem real. The voice of reason is there, but the voice of the addict is stronger. My addiction was certainly powerful, and my dad's nagging just triggered my denial. Sometimes, it even made me forget how much I hated being a smoker. Instead, I vowed that if I ever succeeded in quitting, I would never become a fanatical ex-smoker. The desire to quit, I knew even then, had to come from within.

It wasn't that I didn't want to quit. I tried everything: Acupuncture, hypnosis, tapering off, cold turkey, smoking cessation books and classes, vitamin therapy, special diets, and lots of raw determination. The number of quit attempts I made might indicate that nothing worked. In fact, everything worked, at least for a little while. I would succeed, sometimes for as much as a month or two, but sooner or later I would hit a crisis, and anxiety or depression would send me racing to the local convenience store. Every single time I started up again, I experienced such a sense of failure that I scarcely felt worthy to live. Nevertheless, I kept smoking and kept wishing with every fiber of my being that I could quit.

In 1989, a close family friend died of lung cancer. A few days after his death, I quit smoking again and this time stayed away from cigarettes for almost five months. But this time I recognized something that would later prove important: My feelings of depression intensified when I didn't smoke. When I started smoking again, I felt able to cope. Though I didn't understand the connection then, the first studies on the link between depression and nicotine dependence were already under way. It would take the scientific community many more years to realize the importance of that link, but I knew there was some kind of internal chemistry going on over which I had no control. I still wanted to quit, though, and kept looking for an opportunity to make it happen.

Such an opportunity presented itself soon afterward. I had gone back to college and was a full-time student at the University of Southern Colorado. My major, mass communications, required coursework in advertising. For one of those classes, I wrote a paper about the effectiveness of tobacco ads, focusing on the Joe Camel campaign that had helped RJ Reynolds enjoy a bonanza in profits with the once-moribund Camel cigarettes brand. The research I did for this paper uncovered the loathsome tactics tobacco companies use to hook kids and once again inspired my desire to quit. But I couldn't forget all the times I'd tried and failed. I sat down one day and counted the times I'd attempted to quit. I could hardly believe it when I realized that I had sincerely tried to quit smoking eleven times! Bloody but unbowed, I decided to go for an even dozen. But this time I sought help from my family physician.

I leveled with my doctor. I told him about all the times I'd tried to quit and the many methods I'd used. I felt that I had exhausted every possibility.

"I'll try anything," I said. "I'll take tranquilizers, I'll try nicotine gum, I'll even undergo torture if I have to, but please help me, Doctor. I'm desperate!"

My doctor looked thoughtful. "I've had a few patients who've had some success with nicotine gum, but it seems to cause stomach upset in some people. There's something new, though, that's just come out. A sales representative from a pharmaceutical company dropped off a couple of samples a few days ago. It's a transdermal patch that delivers a controlled dose of nicotine through the skin."

I had never heard of it. "Does it work?" was all I wanted to know.

"It's been thoroughly tested, but I've never prescribed it before. Would you like to be my guinea pig?"

I was stunned at the price of this new therapy: My first dose cost almost $200. And that was just the first month's supply! I would have to stay on the patch for three whole months. Still, I was ready to try anything. So I plunked down my money and slapped a patch on my upper arm. To my delight and relief, it worked. And at that price, it should have!

I wore the patch faithfully for ninety days. The side effects included bizarre dreams and irritated skin at the patch site. I solved the first problem by removing the patch at night. I had never smoked first thing upon awakening, so this worked for me. As for the skin irritation, I solved that problem by moving the patch to different sites each day. The slight itching I still experienced seemed a small price to pay for the benefits it brought. Not once during those three months did I feel a strong desire for a cigarette. I developed new habits and coping skills during those months. But when I went off the patch, I was again troubled by anxiety and depression. I also began suffering from insomnia, which had plagued me off and on since childhood. One reason for my depression was that I was going through a divorce, but these feelings had hit me every single time I'd quit. This time, however, I was determined not to let anything lead me back to smoking. Instead, I returned to my doctor.

"What you're describing is classic depression," said my doctor. "I think it has a lot more to do with what's going on in your life than with giving up cigarettes, but let's try a mild dose of antidepressants and see how you do."

I started on a low dose of antidepressants, which were later adjusted to higher levels. Within two weeks, the anxiety attacks disappeared. I started sleeping at night, and my depression lifted. Months passed, and I was able to resist the urge to smoke. After a year, I realized that I had made it. I had become a nonsmoker.

A few years after I quit smoking, I went to work for the Colorado Dental Association. One of my responsibilities was the management of an educational program for children about the oral health hazards of chewing tobacco. Called the Quit the Spit Project, it was modeled after the spectacularly successful Tar Wars program that had been developed by a Denver physician who thought the only way to solve the problem of tobacco-related deaths was to prevent kids from ever starting.

But Quit the Spit was a dull echo of Tar Wars. When I inherited the project, there were a dozen dentist volunteers giving unimaginative slide-show presentations to schoolchildren in rural communities in northeastern Colorado. Though the emphasis was on chewing tobacco, essentially it was the same old tobacco prevention message I'd heard when I was in school—and I knew how well that had worked! I decided to revamp the program to make it more interesting and, I hoped, more relevant to kids. I jazzed up the script, created new slides with colorful cartoon characters (shades of Joe Camel), and repackaged the program with additional materials that included more emphasis on the oral health hazards of smoking as well as of chewing tobacco.

Remembering how little I'd been impressed by pictures of tarry lungs and cancerous cells, I concentrated on the cosmetic hazards, such as bad breath and stained teeth, thereby hitting kids where it really hurt: right in their vanity. I also looked for celebrity endorsements. We were delighted when Mike Shanahan, head coach of the Denver Broncos, allowed us to use his name and image to promote the idea that tobacco use was incompatible with being a winner. The combined result was a powerful emotional punch that launched the program like a brushfire on an open prairie. Within six months, the twelve volunteers had grown to more than one hundred. Two years later, we had franchises in eleven other states. When it moved into Canada in 1996, the Quit the Spit Project became international.

Thanks to Quit the Spit, I became involved with my state's tobacco control movement. This later led to a job with the American Cancer Society. Among my responsibilities was the development of a train-the-trainer program for smoking cessation facilitators, which eventually became the *You Can Quit*™ program. Many of my students in these training sessions were doctors, nurses, pharmacists, and other health care professionals who understood the physiology of smoking but hadn't a clue how to convince patients to change this destructive behavior. I watched tobacco control activists try to cope with dramatic increases in youth smoking. I also talked to hundreds of relatives and friends of tobacco users who called in despair, saying, "I'm frightened for my son/daughter/brother/sister/husband/wife. What can I do to help them quit?" I searched for answers, but among the available literature was nothing for people who cared about smokers. All I could find were more terrifying health statistics. And the family and friends of smokers were already well aware of those.

It soon became apparent that for every smoker who called our office seeking help to quit, at least five relatives or friends called searching for some magic formula that would succeed where they had failed. As I struggled to help these desperate individuals, it occurred to me that we were aiming our efforts at the wrong people. We were focusing on tobacco users, nearly all of whom are in some form of denial. But there are people who are in a position to help these addicts in ways the uninvolved observer can't. The problem is that these people don't know how to help. They struggle along in ignorance, making the same mistakes my father made: nagging, pleading, using threats, and quoting health statistics. As I know only too well, this doesn't work. Nevertheless, through constant searching and access to some of the best scientific knowledge available, I stumbled upon methods that *do* appear to have a positive impact. These are the methods I want to share with you.

Experience has taught me that it's futile to force change in other people. But it *is* possible to alter your own behavior, thereby creating an atmosphere that is conducive to change. The methods I recommend to family and friends of smokers can be summarized in the response that one of my Quit the Spit dentists gave to an elementary school student who said, "My mom smokes and I'm afraid she's going to die. What can I do?"

The dentist replied, "Tell your mother that you love her. And when she's ready to quit, give her all the support and encouragement you can."

Naturally, it's a little more complicated than that. But before we delve into the complexities, let's find out why people start smoking and why it's so very hard to quit.

ᕫ Chapter Two ᕬ

UNDERSTANDING WHY PEOPLE SMOKE—AND WHY IT'S SO HARD TO QUIT

I once received a letter from a man who objected to the resources the American Cancer Society spends on tobacco control.

"I've watched two family members and four good friends die of emphysema and cancer," he wrote. "All of them stopped smoking about the time they had to go on oxygen. None had any apparent problems quitting. My contention is that they could have stopped anytime if they wanted to. Their deaths had as much to do with a lack of personal discipline and responsibility as anything else."

This is the prevailing attitude in our society: "If people really want to quit smoking, they can do it. . . . It's a question of personal responsibility. . . . Anyone can quit. . . . All it takes is a little discipline."

How I wish this were true.

If it were only a matter of desire, willpower, or responsibility, it would be easy to kick the habit. But for many people, it takes a lot more than discipline. It also takes knowledge, persistence, a willingness to change, and, ideally, the support and understanding of caring family and friends.

This is a book for people who care about someone who smokes. It's also for people who care about protecting themselves from secondhand smoke. This book will guide you through techniques that can help the smoker you care about, but it can also do a great deal to help *you*. Not only can you preserve and perhaps even improve your relationship with the smoker you care about, but you will also learn how to effect changes that include defending yourself against the dangerous toxins in cigarette smoke.

Just How Bad Is Smoking?

Smoking is at least as bad as you think it is—and probably a whole lot worse.

Most people underestimate the negative effects of smoking, none more so than smokers themselves. A survey published in the *Journal of the American Medical Association* (JAMA) reported that most smokers don't believe they run a higher-than-average risk of heart disease or cancer. The more cigarettes smoked, the less likely the smoker was to appreciate the dangers.[1]

But if smokers are in denial, few nonsmokers have any better grasp of reality. People consistently point to alcohol, marijuana, cocaine, crack, heroin, car accidents, homicide, and suicide as some of the most serious problems faced by society. Tobacco is hardly ever mentioned in the same breath as these threats. In fact, tobacco kills more people than alcohol (including drunk driving), cocaine, crack, heroin, marijuana, car accidents, homicide, suicide, fires, and AIDS . . . combined.[2]

A special 1999 edition of *Newsweek* reported that the number one health concern of American women was breast cancer.[3] Ironically, breast cancer isn't even the number one cause of cancer death in women—lung cancer is—and 90 percent of lung cancers are directly attributable to smoking. One-third of all cancer deaths are caused by tobacco, including cancers of the lung, mouth, larynx, throat, stomach, cervix, bladder, and colon. Smoking is a major risk factor for cardiovascular disease, the number one killer of both men and women. It's also the primary cause of emphysema and a significant contributor to numerous respiratory illnesses, including asthma and chronic bronchitis.[4]

What is it about smoking that makes it so deadly? For one thing, tobacco is a fragile plant. To keep it alive until it can be harvested, pesticides and other chemicals must be used. Additional chemicals are added when the tobacco is processed. When these chemicals are burned together with the crushed, dried tobacco leaves, the result is a lethal mixture. Cigarette smoke contains almost five thousand chemicals, including forty-three known cancer-causing agents and four hundred other poisons. One out of every three tobacco users will eventually succumb to its deadly effects.[5]

Think for a minute: If someone were to produce a hair dye that killed one-third of its consumers, how fast would we yank that product off the shelves? Imagine the hue and cry against the airlines if three jumbo jets were to crash, leaving no survivors, every single day for a year. Hard to imagine? The reality is this: If three jumbo jets were to crash every single day, leaving no survivors, the death toll still would not exceed the deaths caused by tobacco.

Keep in mind that these are not "natural" deaths. They are preventable tragedies. But tobacco has a unique distinction. It's a legal product that, when used exactly the way it's intended to be used, kills.

Why People Start Smoking

So why, in light of these numbing statistics, would anyone start smoking in the first place? Most people make the decision to start smoking before they're old enough to know better. Few people start smoking after they become adults. Almost 90 percent of smokers become daily users by the time they're eighteen. More than 60 percent start before the age of fourteen. Most kids start with the idea that they can quit whenever they feel like it. Few see themselves as thirty-year-old smokers. But by the time they graduate from high school, the majority of smoking teenagers already regret their decision. Among smokers age twelve to seventeen years old, 70 percent wish they hadn't started. Nearly as many claim they would like to quit. Only 1 percent of teens who try to quit smoking succeed.[6]

Risky Business

Okay, they're not really old enough to know better. But surely they're not blind, deaf, and dumb. You can frighten a four-year-old into staying away from a hot stove and expect obedience. So why, in spite of the obvious risks, do kids start smoking in the first place? In many cases, kids actually start smoking *because* of the risks. According to the U.S. Department of Health and Human Services (DHHS), the age at which most kids become daily tobacco users is thirteen.[7] Thirteen, as most people would agree, is hardly the Age of Reason. A lot of kids start smoking for the same reason they drive too fast and engage in other dangerous behaviors. A study in Georgia demonstrated that risky driving behavior was the most frequent cause of teenage death and injury due to motor vehicle accidents. If we were to compile a personality profile of the typical teenage smoker, most would probably qualify as risk takers.[8] This is why traditional scare tactics, which most health agencies still employ to convince kids not to start smoking, don't work.

The breathing lung displays at health fairs and lectures about the health consequences of smoking affect only a small percentage of young people. In my opinion, health groups have erred cata-strophically by concentrating on the health risks of smoking be-cause this emphasis appears to have had a boomerang effect with young people. Kids start smoking *because* it's dangerous. They start smoking *because* it's risky and daring. Then, once they start, denial sets in. Talk to a typical teenage smoker, and he'll tell you he plans to quit someday. If not, he'll beat the odds. The average thirteen-year-old is convinced he'll never die or grow old. After all, things like lung cancer and emphysema only happen to old people, right? We're seeing a disturbing increase in tobacco-related illness among younger adults, particularly those who started smoking in their early teens or younger. Nevertheless, to a thirteen-year-old, even thirty is a distant horizon he has a hard time imagining. It's just too distant to seem real.

Youth smoking rates are now at an all-time high. In 1991, one out of seven high school students admitted to being a daily smoker.

By 1994, one out of four high school students smoked every day. Today, it's more than one in three.[9] Every single day, three thousand American kids start smoking.[10] These young smokers replace the smokers who quit or die prematurely from smoking-related diseases. Without them, the tobacco industry would have gone out of business long ago.

Remember, most of these new smokers make the decision to start at around thirteen years of age. Even if he commits a serious crime, a thirteen-year-old is not held accountable the way adults usually are. Thirteen-year-olds cannot legally enter into contractual agreements or even have their ears pierced in most states without their parents' permission. But a thirteen-year-old who starts smoking nearly always does so without parental consent. And a thirteen-year-old who starts smoking is probably making a lifetime commitment.

Sense of Self

Another important feature of our typical teenage smoker is low self-esteem. A thirteen-year-old is just starting to develop her self-image. She is at that awkward age when she's straddling the fence between childhood and adulthood. Although it might be obvious to everyone else, it's often a matter of doubt to her which side of that fence she's going to land on. To the average thirteen-year-old, adults appear to have it all: They come and go as they please, eat and drink what they want, stay up as late as they like, choose their own friends, and are in control of their lives. This, of course, is rarely true, at least of the adults I know. But to an adolescent, adulthood has all the elements of the Good Life. So just as younger children love to imitate their parents, young adolescents continue to imitate what they perceive as adult behavior. Smoking is one behavior that makes them feel like adults.

The problem of youth smoking has given rise to a number of theories to explain it, ranging from rebellion and identity formation to a lack of adult role models and the breakdown of the family unit. There's little agreement about the actual causes of youth smoking, but one thing we do know is that today's kids require a high degree of stimulation. From television to video games to the Internet, today's kids are accustomed to having their desires instantly gratified. Nicotine takes only seconds to reach the brain when inhaled through the lungs. Gratification, therefore, is instantaneous. Cigarettes are also relatively inexpensive and easy for kids to obtain, either through purchase or theft. These combined factors make cigarettes an ideal drug of choice for young people.

Seduction by the Tobacco Industry

The tobacco industry understands the adolescent need for independence and control, and the fragile development of self-esteem that for many, if not most, young people is a painful struggle. It's a vulnerable age, and tobacco companies have exploited it shamelessly. Not only do they focus their advertising in so-called adult magazines with large youth readerships (for example, *Spin, Cycle World, Rolling Stone, People, Mademoiselle, Glamour,* and *Cosmopolitan,* which all promote youth themes of glamour, fun, independence, and excitement), but also they clearly recognize a young person's need for adult role models.

Anyone who saw the hit movie *My Best Friend's Wedding* probably remembers Julia Roberts's character chain-smoking. The brand she smoked, Marlboro, was prominently displayed in the film. In all likelihood, this was no accident. Tobacco companies have historically paid huge sums to producers, directors, actors, and screenwriters so their brands would be featured in films and television shows. These payments, known as product placement fees, were outlawed by a 1998 settlement between the tobacco industry and attorneys general from forty-six states, but the practice continues in Hollywood, often for obscure artistic reasons not obvious to the general public.

Another feature of the tobacco settlement was to outlaw the locating of tobacco billboards near schools and playgrounds. The industry is further prohibited from distributing specialty items carrying tobacco company logos, such as hats, T-shirts, gym bags, and water bottles, at rock concerts and other places frequented by young people; however, free product samples (for example, chewing tobacco) are still passed out at rodeos and stock shows and offered through magazine and Internet ads. Kids also manage to obtain cigarettes from vending machines and stores, even those where clerks wear buttons proclaiming, "We ID everyone with the purchase of tobacco products."

It's against the law to sell tobacco products to anyone under the age of eighteen. But sales of tobacco to minors occur all the time. In one sting operation by Project ASSIST (American Stop Smoking Intervention Study) in my hometown of Aurora, Colorado, underage kids recruited for the operation were each given $1. They were then instructed to enter randomly selected convenience stores and told to try to buy a pack of cigarettes with their dollar. In most stores, the kids were either asked for ID or turned away when they admitted that all they had was a dollar. But in one case, *a clerk actually took money out of her own pocket to make up the difference!* It's also commonplace for enterprising high school students who have already turned eighteen to sell "loosies," individual cigarettes from packs they've purchased legally, to younger classmates. This practice is seldom monitored or penalized, especially in places where parents and school authorities do not regard tobacco as a dangerous drug.

The attitudes of most new users are formed long before they try their first cigarette or their first pinch of chewing tobacco, and advertising has traditionally influenced the way kids view tobacco. One example of this type of influence is Joe Camel, an ad campaign RJ Reynolds jettisoned after antitobacco activists complained that Joe was more recognizable to preschoolers than Mickey Mouse or Ronald McDonald. Another promotion that worked extremely well from a marketing perspective until it was banned by the tobacco settlement was bubble gum in chewing tobacco packaging and candy cigarettes with actual cigarette brand logos.

Pointedly missing from the tobacco settlement were point-of-sale ads and displays in convenience and discount stores. Known as "slot marketing" or "slotting," these easy-to-reach displays make it easy for kids to steal cigarettes that conscientious clerks might refuse to sell them. For placing these displays in strategic locations, tobacco companies pay the owners of convenience and retail stores enormous fees, which more than make up for any profit they might lose to theft. These payments are a good investment in the future for the tobacco companies. They know they'll recoup their investment later on, once their replacement customers are good and properly hooked.

Why People Continue to Smoke

The addictive properties of nicotine are so powerful and, in many cases, so immediate, that all tobacco companies have to do is get kids to try their products, and they're practically guaranteed a lifetime customer. Repeat business, as any good salesperson knows, is where businesses make most of their money. And nicotine makes cigarettes a marketer's dream. Smokers have been known to put cigarettes ahead of food when economic factors force them to make a choice. Later on, they may even put them ahead of survival when the cumulative effects of smoking catch up with them.

Inhaled smoke carries nicotine deep into the lungs, where it is absorbed into the bloodstream. Nicotine affects many parts of the body, including the cardiovascular system, the hormonal system, and the brain. Nicotine changes the way the brain relays information by inhibiting the flow of information between nerve cells. As their nervous systems adapt, smokers gradually increase the number of cigarettes, which increases the amount of nicotine in the blood. Eventually, a smoker reaches a target level and then smokes to maintain nicotine at this level.[11] It is at this point that smoking becomes a compulsion rather than a choice. This is when smokers become addicted.

The absence of nicotine leads to withdrawal symptoms that force smokers to smoke more to boost levels of nicotine in the bloodstream back to the target level. It's the same thing that happens to heroin addicts. Think of a cigarette as a hypodermic needle and you'll have a much better idea of what smokers are actually doing every single time they inhale.

Smoking is not only physically addicting, it's also psychologically addicting, or habit forming. To demonstrate, let's do some simple arithmetic. The average smoker consumes one to one and a half packs a day. Twenty cigarettes are in a pack. It takes at least ten hits, or inhalations, to finish a cigarette. Each time a smoker places a cigarette between his lips and draws smoke into his lungs, he is performing an individual act of smoking. And he is doing this *two to three hundred times a day!*

Tell me, what conscious acts do you perform two to three hundred times every single day of your life? Probably nothing, right? Consider the fact that habits tend to be reinforced by repetition, and you'll have a pretty good idea why the smoking habit becomes so much a part of the smoker's life. Combine this with a powerful physical addiction, and you'll have a better understanding of why it's so difficult to quit smoking.

Hard-Core Smokers

Chances are, the smoker you care about started when she was very young. Chances are even better that she's tried to quit, perhaps many times. Some smokers find it easy. They just set their cigarettes aside and never look back. These people are in the minority. If the smoker you care about were one of them, you probably wouldn't be reading this book.

Most people find quitting very hard. Some find it close to impossible. These are the smokers those of us in the tobacco control business refer to as hard-core smokers. I was one of these. The smoker you care about may also be one. The characteristics of hard-core smokers include:

- Suffer from "blue moods" or other symptoms of depression
- Started smoking before age eighteen
- Tried to quit at least once and probably several times
- Hang out with other smokers (most friends, co-workers, or both smoke)
- Suffer from low self-esteem

- Often smoke first thing upon awakening in the morning
- Continue to smoke despite increasing health problems, social ostracism, or both
- Deny that smoking is harming them, even when obviously it is
- May exhibit risk-taking behavior
- May have a history of mental illness, other substance abuse, or both

If the smoker you care about fits most of these characteristics, chances are he is a hard-core smoker. He probably doesn't want to smoke. He may not even like smoking but can't seem to stop, no matter how hard or how often he tries. One reason it's so difficult is that addiction forces smokers into denial. Hard-core smokers hear the evidence about the health risks of smoking. They understand that smoking is dangerous. But addicts force the message to undergo a transformation. By the time it filters through to the smoker's consciousness, it somehow becomes redirected toward that vague group of *others* who smoke. The messages are never directed at the smoker because smoking is not hurting him.

Sometimes hard-core smokers can even convince themselves of this after they've developed emphysema, heart disease, or lung cancer. My maternal grandfather continued to smoke long after he was diagnosed with emphysema. I used to marvel at his ability to argue that the cause of his illness was all the dust he'd inhaled during his years as a farmer on the plains of eastern Colorado. Usually, he made these arguments between hacking coughs while puffing on a cigarette, pausing every now and then to refresh himself from the oxygen tank tucked away in a corner. Truly, the human mind is an amazing vehicle.

For years, the tobacco industry has claimed that smokers fully comprehend the dangers of smoking. We now know this simply isn't true. A survey by the University of California at Berkeley showed that the heaviest smokers tend to be overly optimistic about their chances of living to be seventy-five years of age or more.[12] Other studies have shown that heavy smokers as a group tend to speed more and use seat belts less often than nonsmokers, which indicates that hard-core smokers are either in denial about the risks of smoking or they're not good at judging risk in general.

Other variables besides denial contribute to low quit-smoking rates. Among these are high nicotine dependency (smokers who report severe withdrawal symptoms during previous quit attempts); low motivation or readiness to change; a perceived inability to quit; and stressful life circumstances or a recent life change such as a new job or a divorce. Psychiatric factors may also be present. Someone who suffers from depression, schizophrenia, attention deficit hyperactivity disorder (ADHD), alcoholism, or other chemical dependencies will probably find it very hard to quit smoking.

But even if these conditions are present, the situation is far from hopeless. Every one of the variables mentioned above can be overcome with medical treatment, counseling, and the understanding and support of family and friends. By approaching your smoker with compassion rather than anger, with understanding rather than blame, and by giving her the tools she needs to break this dangerous addiction, *you* can mean the difference between success and failure to the smoker you care about.

You may even mean the difference between life and death.

☙ Chapter Three ❧

THE STAGES OF CHANGE

Very few smokers wake up one morning and shout, "Eureka! I finally understand that smoking is bad for me! Now that I know, I believe I'll quit!" It would be nice if it were so easy to recognize when a smoker is ready to quit. Unfortunately, this is rarely the case.

Most smokers go through a number of stages on the road to change. These stages were first identified by James Prochaska and Carlo DiClemente of the University of Rhode Island in the late 1970s. This has since become the accepted model for a broad range of behavioral changes, including overcoming alcohol and drug addiction, losing weight, and stopping smoking.

Some people move from one stage to the next in a fairly orderly fashion. Some bounce back and forth like a bewildered rubber ball. Still others embark upon their journey at the end, amble back toward the beginning, and end up somewhere halfway in between. Your ability to recognize the various twists, turns, and potholes along this road can help steer your smoker toward a safer, healthier future.

The desire to change generally begins with:

1. **The Precognitive or Precontemplative Stage:** It's possible that your smoker is at this stage right now. He may deny that smoking is harmful, at least to him. She may claim that she enjoys smoking and plans to go on doing so even if it kills her. He may point to role models like

the late George Burns who smoked cigars but lived to be one hundred. (Burns actually smoked few of those cigars; mostly, he used them as stage props.) She may be hostile or belligerent when you bring up the subject of smoking. A smoker in the precontemplative stage will probably resent going outdoors to smoke and may roll his eyes when you talk about the dangers of passive smoking. All of these are examples of denial.

Smokers in this stage are not open to change. It's pointless to badger them about quitting. But keep in mind that most smokers really do want to quit. Those who claim they don't often are reacting to the frustration of previous failed quit attempts. Or they may simply be sick and tired of people trying to force, trick, chide, or browbeat them into doing something they're not ready to do. Be patient. In all likelihood, a day will come when they genuinely want to quit.

2. **The Cognitive or Contemplative Stage:** During this stage, the smoker begins to think about quitting. This may occur when a relative, friend, or acquaintance dies of lung cancer or emphysema. It might come about as a result of a hike in cigarette prices, new clean-indoor-air policies, or some other factor that demonstrates the inconvenience of smoking. They're not yet ready to quit, but they are receptive to information about quitting.

Smokers in this stage may talk about quitting. He has not yet taken action, but the desire is there. During this stage smokers are receptive to encouragement. This is a great time to build your smoker's self-esteem. Do all you can to empower your smoker, help him overcome his fear of failure, and help raise his confidence in his ability to beat the smoking addiction.

3. **The Determination or Preparation Stage:** During this stage, smokers may begin to investigate stop-smoking classes or calculate the cost of Zyban, nicotine replacement therapy, and other stop-smoking aids. She may set

a quit date or start buying cigarettes by the pack instead of the carton. This is the time to educate your smoker about some of the myths that have kept her tied to cigarettes and the time to learn all you can about innovative stop-smoking treatments. It's also a great time to start practicing some of the healthful living guidelines outlined in this book. Even if your smoker never quits, these guidelines will improve her health and may encourage her to cut down on the number of cigarettes she smokes.

4. **The Action Stage:** This occurs when smokers actually throw their cigarettes away. It includes everything from the quit date to six months after quitting. In this stage, your smoker may be highly motivated but still needs your support. This is the time to be on guard against other smokers who, unconsciously or consciously, may try to sabotage your ex-smoker's quit attempt. It's also time to prepare for emergency situations that may inspire the "just one won't hurt" mentality that leads so many ex-smokers back to smoking.

5. **The Maintenance Stage:** This is the period from six months to five years after quitting. During this stage, the person you care about is still an ex-smoker. He isn't really considered a nonsmoker until he has been smoke-free for five or more years. The reason for this is that the relapse rate remains relatively high throughout those first five years, though the risk gradually lessens the longer he remains smoke-free. It only takes about three to five days for an ex-smoker's system to purge itself of nicotine, but it takes considerably longer for smokers to develop new coping skills to replace habits they've traditionally associated with smoking. For some smokers, it may take years before they feel comfortable without cigarettes. Don't be surprised if your ex-smoker appears despondent or experiences down feelings during this stage. If these feelings are prolonged or severe, consider

the link between smoking and depression and encourage your ex-smoker to get treatment for depression.

6. **The Relapse Stage:** Hopefully, this is a stage neither you nor your ex-smoker will ever have to deal with. But if it happens, don't give way to despair. Most smokers quit many times before they finally succeed. I stand here today, a nonsmoker after eleven failed quit attempts, as living proof that a single relapse does not equal ultimate failure.

Wherever smokers happen to be at every stage of the quitting process, it's important to celebrate where they are. Quitting is hard work, but always remember that the heavy lifting is up to the quitters. You can offer support, be a sounding board, even help smooth the way, but they're the ones who have to do the hard work. Your primary role is to sit on the sidelines and cheer them on.

How to Help the Smoker You Care about Quit

To effect change, you must first accept that it can't be forced. Unless the smoker you care about is ready to quit or has at least started thinking about quitting, none of your pearls of wisdom nor all your tears and lamentations will have the slightest impact. In fact, with the wrong approach, your irresistible force is likely to meet an immovable object and may even harden your smoker's resolve to continue smoking.

As you read through the following steps, remember that however much you might wish it, however diligently you try, if the smoker you care about doesn't want to quit, he or she won't do it. If, in spite of all your efforts, the smoker you care about continues to smoke, you may simply have to accept it. This may be hard news to take, but the one and only person you can change is yourself. The overriding principle behind every one of these steps is self-change. It is not about changing another person.

Changing yourself, however, can lead to change in others. Everything we do has a domino effect. One action invariably leads to a reaction. That is the secret behind everything in this book.

I firmly believe there is no such thing as a disposable person. This effort is worth a try, if for no other reason than to preserve your relationship with the smoker you care about. So read on.

Step 1: Don't Nag! (Precontemplative)
Step 2: Redirect Your Anger (Precontemplative)
Step 3: Clear the Air (Precontemplative)
Step 4: Empower Your Smoker (Contemplative)
Step 5: Overcome the Fear of Failure (Contemplative)
Step 6: Focus on the Present (Preparation)
Step 7: Explore Stop-Smoking Treatments (Preparation)
Step 8: Get Physical (Preparation/Action)
Step 9: Food for Thought (Preparation/Action)
Step 10: What to Expect When Your Smoker Quits (Action)
Step 11: Find Birds of a Different Feather for Your Smoker to Flock With (Action)
Step 12: Driving on the Wrong Side of the Road (Maintenance)
Step 13: Consider the Link between Smoking and Depression (Maintenance)
Step 14: Celebrate Where You Are (Relapse)

❦ Part II ❧

✎ Introduction ✐

This section begins the actual steps involved in helping someone you care about quit smoking. These fourteen steps follow the basic Prochaska-DiClemente model. They incorporate scientifically tested methods for quitting smoking and proven communication techniques to motivate your smoker. But don't be surprised if you find one or more of these steps inappropriate for your circumstances or relationship. Based upon my knowledge and experience, I've tried to cover as many contingencies as possible, but every circumstance is different. You know your smoker better than I do, and if you honestly feel that any of the suggestions in this book will have a negative impact on your smoker, by all means skip that step and move on to the next one. Nothing that is written here is either cast in stone or divinely inspired. I've never been much of a stickler for rules, especially when rules get in the way of achieving an important goal.

Whenever I conduct train-the-trainer sessions, I always tell my facilitators to tailor their stop-smoking programs to the needs of their participants. By the same token, be creative in adapting these steps to your own needs and those of your smoker. Try to use good judgment and avoid anything manipulative or controlling. Above all, keep in mind that this isn't about forcing others to dance to your tune. *It's about inspiring change by first changing yourself.*

It might help to conduct periodic self-assessments at various points along the way to make sure *you're* not stuck in a precontemplative mode. Keep moving forward, and always remember, the only real failure is the failure to try.

ꙮ Chapter Four ꙮ

STEP 1: DON'T NAG!
Precontemplative Stage

If you have children, think back to their first words. Chances are they learned to say "Da Da" or "Ma Ma" early in life. But no sooner had they identified you when they learned to say "no!" to just about everything you asked them to do. It is a rare youngster who does not regard the word "no!" as one of the handiest in his vocabulary. See if the following dialogue rings any bells:

"Pick up your toys, Billy."

"*No!*"

"Time for bed, Susie."

"*No!*"

"Eat your broccoli, Tommy."

"*No!*"

Sound familiar? Now, let's try the same theme with a different cast of characters:

"Smoking is so bad for you, Bill/Sue/Tom. Won't you please quit?"

"*I'll quit someday. Get off my back, won't you?*" *(Translation: "No!")*

Remember the profile of our typical teenage smoker? Rebellion was an element of that profile. This goes back to the reasons your smoker started smoking in the first place. Keep in mind that a lot of kids start smoking not in spite of the risk but *because* of it.

Risk-taking behavior is exciting and daring to many adolescents. It's a way of breaking the rules and testing the structures of the adult world. Many kids regard smoking as an act of defiance. By embracing a known risk, they demonstrate their ability not only to cheat death but also to challenge the authority whose control they wish to escape. It's a form of mutiny many kids view as a hallmark of independence.

There's still a trace of that mutinous teenager in the smoker you care about. Here's proof: How does your smoker react when you nag her about quitting? Chances are, she reacts with anger or defiance, which she may express in one of three ways:

1. Verbal defiance ("Get off my back!")
2. Symbolic defiance (lights a cigarette and blows the smoke in your face)
3. Passive-aggressive defiance (agrees to quit but continues to smoke in secret)

Every smoker I've ever known has told me that being nagged about quitting only increases the desire to smoke. Nagging triggers old subconscious roles. When you nag, you assume the role of authoritarian parent. The smoker once again becomes an insecure youth, wanting more control of his life. The desire to smoke in this situation is automatic. Obviously, this is the exact opposite of the behavior you're hoping to inspire.

It's also futile to hide cigarettes, break up packs you find lying around, flush cigarettes down the toilet, or any variation of this theme. This is a popular ploy with children whose parents smoke. In the belief that out of sight means out of mind, they try to trick Mom or Dad into quitting by removing the source of temptation. These kids have my heartfelt sympathy. So does anyone else desperate enough to try something like this. But these methods are worse than ineffective. They are likely to inspire tremendous anger in the smoker you care about. Anger causes stress. And we know what smokers do when they're stressed, don't we? That's right—they smoke more!

These tactics do nothing but create negative energy in your smoker. It makes her feel defensive, guilty, and helpless. It triggers all the insecurities of childhood. It may even kill the desire to quit. Nobody likes to be told what to do. And forcing a behavioral change is not what you're trying to accomplish. You want to make the smoker your ally. After all, you're trying to help her, aren't you? The trick is to convince her that you're on her side, not browbeat her into dancing to your tune.

You're probably thinking, "Well, if I don't nag, he will keep smoking forever." On the contrary, I am absolutely convinced that no smoker ever quit because somebody nagged him into it. It is basic human nature to desire some sense of control or mastery over circumstances, and smokers are no exception. The smoker you care about may agree to quit, or even pretend to quit just to shut you up, but sooner or later he'll return to his old friend nicotine. His need to be in control demands it.

The real difficulty arises when you don't realize you're nagging. See what your response is to the following questions:

1. Do you seize any opportunity to mention that the smoker you care about is still smoking (as if, somehow, she were unaware of it)?
2. Do you complain about the smell, the expense, or the inconvenience of smoking whenever you have an opportunity to do so?
3. Do you clip articles about the health risks of smoking and shove them in your smoker's face or even read them out loud?
4. Do you look for opportunities to remind your smoker of the damage she's doing to herself, her family, and her belongings by continuing to smoke?
5. Do you inevitably bring the conversation back to smoking, even when the topic under discussion is something totally unrelated?
6. Do you constantly urge the smoker you care about to quit?

If you answered yes to any of these questions, chances are good the smoker you care about thinks you're nagging, even if you don't think so yourself. If you even suspect you might be nagging, consider your own feelings when somebody nags you about bad habits you may have acquired. Chances are, it doesn't inspire you to stop the behavior. If anything, it only makes you angry or resentful toward the person who is nagging you.

I know that nagging is a difficult habit to break. In fact, it's almost as difficult to stop nagging as it is to stop smoking. But by continuing to nag, all you are doing is prolonging the desire to smoke. Take my word for it, there are better ways of motivating the decision to quit.

Advice columnist Abigail Van Buren ("Dear Abby") once likened being nagged to being nibbled to death by a duck. The decision to quit has to come from the smoker. All you can do is offer support and wait until your smoker makes the decision to quit on his own.

ඞ Chapter Five ඲

STEP 2: REDIRECT YOUR ANGER
Precontemplative Stage

When someone you care about smokes, you may feel a lot of anger. Some of this is probably tied to a fear of loss. With awareness of the death and suffering caused by tobacco, it's natural to fear for someone you care about. Fear and anger are close cousins. But anger can be counterproductive, even destructive, unless it's properly channeled. If you've always believed, as most people do, that smoking is an act of free will, your anger has probably been focused on the smoker. This is a normal reaction to grief, or anticipation of grief. How could he be so selfish as to risk his life with a substance that everyone knows will kill him? How could she care so little for the pain she will cause once the hazards of smoking catch up with her? And how can you ever forgive him for dying from something that could have been prevented, if only he'd had the strength to quit?

Contrary to tobacco industry propaganda, smoking is rarely an adult choice. Most people start smoking long before they reach adulthood and continue smoking because of powerful psychological and physiological factors. The truth is that most smokers would love to overcome these factors, if only they could. Before you read this book, you may not have known this. If so, you may have expressed anger toward your smoker for his supposed refusal to quit. This, in turn, has probably made him defensive. It might help to know that the motive for this defensiveness is guilt. The vast majority of smokers really want to quit. When they can't, they feel a tremendous sense of failure. Their defensiveness is a mask for that failure.

Psychologists agree that happiness is tied in part to our sense of control. When situations arise that make people feel helpless or out of control, they often respond by putting on a tough face, or pretending they don't care. The more belligerent your smoker is about smoking, the guiltier she probably feels about it. This may not ease your anger, but it might inspire your compassion.

Smokers are like everyone else—they need to feel that the people who care for them are on their side. They also need to feel confidence in their own ability to effect change. But they can't feel this way if they're constantly being attacked. They will do whatever they have to do to defend themselves from further assaults.

At the same time, your anger may be difficult to control. It's hard to watch people you care about doing something you know is bad for them. You and your smoker may have become locked in a vicious cycle of blame and denial, punishment and resentment. But you, as a nonaddict, have more choices. You have the power to break the cycle.

Before you bring up the topic of smoking, consider your own feelings. Try to stay calm enough to consider the situation from the smoker's perspective. If you find yourself getting angry or frustrated because he continues to stonewall, say, "I need to think about that." Then go off by yourself for a while until you calm down.

When you are feeling calm, try redirecting your anger. Stop blaming your smoker for the harm tobacco is doing to her. Instead, blame the tobacco! It's the smoking you hate, not the smoker. If you must vent your frustration on some human object, direct it at the pushers who hooked your smoker in the first place. You would likely feel tremendous rage toward an adult who abused a child. How would you feel about an adult who tempted children with attractively wrapped packages containing arsenic and formaldehyde, or gassed them with carbon monoxide and hydrogen cyanide (which, coincidentally, are just a few of the nearly five thousand chemicals in tobacco smoke)? Your smoker is a victim, not a villain. The villains are those who seduced her into experimenting with tobacco, probably before she was old enough to make an adult choice.

Redirect Your Anger

It's important to learn how to communicate with your smoker. Remember that anger may be a mask for sorrow or fear, or even disappointment at not getting something you want. To communicate these emotions, first redirect your anger by blaming the substance rather than the smoker. Instead of saying, "I hate you for smoking!" say, "I hate tobacco for what it's doing to you." Then express what you want by naming your specific desire. Finally, empower your smoker by expressing positive, loving support. The process works like this:

1. **Redirect your anger:** *"I hate* tobacco for what it's doing to you. *I am so angry* at the industry that seduced you into starting to smoke before you were old enough to understand what it would do to you."

2. **Express your desire:** *"I want* you to stop smoking. *I want* you to live a long, healthy, productive life."

3. **Empower your smoker:** *"I care* for you. *I know* you have the strength to quit smoking. *You deserve* to be free of this addiction."

You may need to practice this technique before you feel comfortable with it. Once you do, you may be surprised to discover what an empowering and energizing effect it has on the smoker you care about. Instead of letting negative thoughts about and fears for your smoker build up, try the communication technique described above and see what happens.

When you express negative feelings, be sure to use "I" words that focus on your feelings rather than "you" words that blame your smoker. Use "you" words only when you're expressing understanding or support. For example:

Don't Say: "Will *you* listen to that cough? *You* sound like the last act of *Camille*. Why are *you* so determined to kill *yourself* with cigarettes?"

Do Say: "*I worry* about that cough. *I want* to see you well and strong. *I care* for you, and *I know* you can quit. *You deserve* to be free of tobacco's control over your life."

Don't Say: "If *you* really cared about me, *you'd* quit smoking."

Do Say: "*I hate* to think of anything bad happening to you. *I know* you're strong enough to quit. When you're ready, *I'll give* you all the support I can because *you really deserve* to be a nonsmoker."

In all likelihood, your smoker wants to quit even more than you want it for him. But he needs encouragement, not blame. He needs support, not carping. Above all, your smoker needs to know you're on his side. Go ahead and express your feelings. But put it in the form of what *you* want or what *you* feel, not what you believe *he's* doing to you. For example:

Don't Say: "You're scaring the hell out of me, you insensitive jerk!"

Do Say: "I feel frightened when I think about the dangers of smoking."

Don't Say: "You make me so angry when you refuse to quit! If you had any willpower, you wouldn't make me suffer this way!"

Do Say: "I would love to help you quit smoking when you're ready."

Do you see the difference? When you express empathy and understanding, your smoker feels secure enough to make the right choices. Just remember, it's the smoker who has to do all the heavy lifting. This is about empowerment. It's about helping your smoker find her own personal source of power so she can free herself from her addiction.

ා Chapter Six ෴

STEP 3: CLEAR THE AIR
Precontemplative Stage

Remember what I said earlier about change? You can't force it on another person. You *can* change yourself. Compassion, understanding, and tolerance are effective tools in helping your smoker quit—up to a point. But you can and need to draw the line when someone is putting your own life or health in jeopardy.

If you spend a lot of time around smokers, you are placing your own health at considerable risk. Secondhand, or passive, smoking is one of the leading causes of preventable death. Every eight smokers who die from smoking take one nonsmoker with them.[1] Smokers' rights groups such as the National Smokers Alliance (which receives most of its funding from the tobacco industry) are vocal about the right of adults to smoke wherever and whenever they choose. I am unaware of any Constitutional right to smoke. The right to breathe, however, is self-evident.

There is evidence that some nonsmokers may be even more susceptible to health problems from cigarette smoke than smokers are. The reason is that smokers develop compensatory responses to some of the poisons in cigarette smoke. Nonsmokers don't have the benefit of these adaptive responses.[2] People with asthma, allergies, respiratory problems, and cardiovascular disease are extremely vulnerable to the harmful elements in secondhand smoke. Heart patients are probably the most vulnerable of all. Many of the fifty-three thousand deaths caused each year by passive smoking are due to heart disease.[3]

There are two types of secondhand smoke. Mainstream smoke is the smoke that smokers exhale; sidestream smoke is the smoke that comes from lit cigarettes. Many poisonous gases are present in very high concentrations in sidestream smoke. Smoke from an "idling" cigarette contains nearly two times the amount of tar and nicotine, up to five times as much carbon monoxide, and fifty times as much ammonia as the smoke that smokers inhale.[4]

So even though you don't smoke and may be doing all the right things for your own health, you're still in danger from tobacco, possibly even more danger than smokers are. Because of this danger, you have every right to insist that the smoker you care about refrain from smoking in your presence. If you're pregnant or if you have children, you actually have an *obligation* to insist upon clean air. Pregnant women exposed to secondhand smoke have more miscarriages and more low-birthweight babies than women who avoid smokers. People who smoke around babies or infants may be contributing to higher rates of sudden infant death syndrome (SIDS), more respiratory problems, more sore throats, more ear infections, and worsening of asthma symptoms.[5] The elderly are also susceptible to problems from secondhand smoke, particularly if they suffer from heart disease or respiratory ailments.

A smoker's addiction often forces him to deny the dangers of tobacco. But you are not addicted. You have no excuses. There is no reason anyone should be permitted to endanger your life and health or the life and health of your children.

By asking smokers not to smoke in your presence, you're doing them a favor even though they may not think so. In fact, they may well express resentment when you insist that they smoke elsewhere. Nevertheless, you should insist, both for your sake and theirs. By making it inconvenient for your smoker to keep smoking, you're actually changing the culture around your smoker. You're making smoking socially unacceptable. You're also making it easier for your smoker to make the difficult decision to quit.

The fact that more work sites and other public places have gone smoke-free is a large factor in declining adult smoking rates. One frequently cited reason for quitting is that there are so few places that permit smoking anymore. A few states and many cities now have laws that ban smoking in public places. In California, this includes bars and casinos, some of the last places most smokers traditionally have been able to pollute the air with impunity. Indeed, the only places where smoking is still allowed without any restrictions are private homes and automobiles, and even these havens are under attack. In 1998, a legislator from my home state of Colorado introduced a bill that would have banned smoking in private cars when children under the age of fifteen were present. Although the bill failed, its sponsor received national attention for her efforts to educate parents about the dangers of secondhand smoke. Lawsuits have been filed against neighbors whose cigarette smoke drifted into non-smokers' apartments or condominiums. It really is just a matter of time before the right to smoke will end where nonsmokers' lungs begin.

By making it more difficult for people to smoke, we are gradually reducing the number of smokers. California, which has some of the nation's toughest smoking restrictions, has one of the nation's lowest smoking rates.[6] Getting these restrictions in place usually involves a battle, but anything that convinces more people to break their addiction to this vicious, deadly drug is worth whatever struggle it entails. It may seem like tough love to many smokers, but one of the most loving things you can do for the smoker you care about is make it harder for her to go on doing something that's killing her.

If you've always permitted the smoker you care about to smoke in your presence, be prepared for resistance when you do an about-face. Don't, however, let this alter your course of action. Simply state that you've become concerned about the effects of second-hand smoke and you'd prefer that he not smoke around you anymore. List some of the statistics you read earlier in this chapter. (It's okay to cite statistics when you're talking about *your* health; smokers are usually in denial only about their own health.) Say that you suffer from nausea or headaches when your smoker smokes (chances are, this is true), and you'd like to see if the absence of cigarette smoke would solve the problem.

If the smoker you care about is someone you live with, ask her to smoke only outdoors. If, for whatever reason, this is not possible, at least restrict smoking to one area of your house or apartment, preferably a well-ventilated area where the smoke can't drift into nonsmoking zones. Make sure it's nowhere near a computer, VCR, or other expensive equipment that can be damaged by the oily film that tobacco smoke leaves behind. (If it does this to your computer, imagine what it's doing to you!) Smoking also damages furniture. In fact, there's not much of anything that stands up well to the ravages of cigarette smoke.

If the smoker you care about doesn't live with you, you have every right to insist that he not smoke in your home. You might also agree to meet him only in public places where smoking isn't allowed. Visiting your smoker in his home may be trickier. The obvious solution is to entertain only at your own house or in places where nonsmoking is the rule, until the smoker has decided to quit. If this is not possible, tell him you will go outdoors every time he lights a cigarette. There is no need to make an issue of this. Simply explain that you will return as soon as the cigarette is out and the smoke has had a chance to clear. Unless the smoker you care about is an inconsiderate clod, your insistence will probably cause fewer cigarettes to be consumed during your visits.

Be prepared for this step to backfire initially. Some smokers may acquiesce without a struggle, but most will fight your decision, either openly and belligerently or in a quiet, passive-aggressive manner. It may be that your smoker will stop accepting your invitations or inviting you to visit. Keep in touch by telephone or e-mail if you have to, but by all means stick to your guns. Never give your smoker permission to smoke when she is with you. By allowing smokers to smoke in your presence, you are granting their addiction tacit approval and endangering your own health in the process.

Adults have the right to make poor choices, but nobody has the right to make other people sick. Your goal is to convince your smoker that breathing isn't optional, not to make it easy or desirable for him to continue smoking. This may be one of the more difficult steps to put into practice, but it's important, not only for your own well-being but also for the ultimate benefit of your smoker. No matter how hard it is, stand your ground and refuse to permit *anyone* to smoke in your presence.

⚘ Chapter Seven ⚘

STEP 4: EMPOWER YOUR SMOKER
Contemplative Stage

Within almost every smoker is a nonsmoker yearning to breathe free. Surveys estimate that at least 70 percent of tobacco users would love to quit if they could. Personally, I think it's higher. Individuals who say they enjoy smoking and don't want to quit are usually kidding themselves. Some of it may be defiance or despair over previous failed quit attempts, because, let's face it, there are so many unpleasant things about smoking, including:

- Awful smell in clothes/hair/auto/home
- Expense
- Mouth sores
- Smoker's cough
- Runny eyes and nose
- More colds, sore throats, and respiratory infections than nonsmokers
- Aging effects on skin
- Yellow teeth, gum disease, and other dental problems
- Cigarette holes in clothes, carpet, furniture, or car
- Running out to the store late at night or other inconvenient times to get cigarettes
- Difficulty exercising or performing athletically
- Cold hands and feet (caused by poor circulation)

- Loss of self-control
- Inability to smell or taste anything
- Inability to sit through a movie, concert, or other social activity where smoking isn't allowed
- Feeling like a social pariah
- Feeling ashamed or despising oneself because of smoking

So, what's to like? Trust me, your smoker wants to quit. Few hard-core smokers really enjoy smoking. They continue to smoke only because they're addicted. They may say they enjoy it. They may even think they enjoy it. But that's because the addict that lives inside your smoker is a liar. Learning to recognize that liar is part of the process of quitting.

Knowing that your smoker wants to quit is important information in your overall strategy. As long as you don't try to force a decision by nagging, thereby triggering defensiveness or denial, smokers are free to embrace this desire of their own free will. All you need to do is gently nurture this natural process along.

In any battle, it's always helpful to know who your allies are. Believe it or not, the smoker you care about is on your side. Become partners in this battle. Don't make the mistake of turning smokers into enemies. You are not at war with *them*. You are at war with tobacco.

Perhaps your smoker is starting to think about quitting, but she's one of those people who claims she likes to smoke. If so, don't challenge this belief. Do, however, ask her what she likes about smoking. Keep your tone nonjudgmental. You're simply asking out of curiosity. She may respond with answers such as:

- It calms me down when I'm uptight.
- It gives me something to do with my hands.
- It keeps me from stuffing my face with food and gaining weight.
- It's my only bad habit.
- It's the only way I reward myself.

Once you know what he likes about smoking, ask if anything else provides the same benefits. For example, ask if your smoker can think of anything else that calms him down when he's uptight or what he does with his hands in situations where he can't smoke. If he can't think of any substitutes, suggest some. For example, to prevent your smoker from overeating when he doesn't smoke, suggest healthy oral substitutes such as sugar-free gum, cinnamon sticks, toothpicks, raw vegetables, and lots of water. We'll get into more specifics about this later, but this will keep him thinking, and that's half the battle.

After your smoker has listed some of the things she likes about smoking, follow up with another question: "Is there anything you don't like about smoking?" (Remember, keep your tone nonjudgmental.) One thing the tobacco control movement *has* accomplished over the past few decades is to tattoo the disadvantages of smoking on everyone's foreheads. Chances are pretty good that most smokers can come up with an entire laundry list of things they *don't* like about smoking. If they can't think of anything, suggest a few of the disadvantages listed above. But do it *gently.* Don't force the issue. Then remind your smoker that you're on her side. Say, "I know you'll quit when you're ready. When you are, remember I'm here to help."

By asking questions, you're accomplishing several things:

- You're reminding your smoker of the reasons for continuing to smoke, which, stated out loud, may seem pointless or silly.
- You're encouraging your smoker to consider substitutes or suggesting substitutes for smoking without forcing the idea of giving up cigarettes.
- You're reminding your smoker about all the negative aspects of smoking as well as some of the reasons your smoker probably wants to quit.
- You're establishing yourself as an ally in the battle to quit.
- You're empowering your smoker by helping him or her come up with solutions.

Don't initiate this discussion in the middle of an argument or when one of you is tired or depressed. But if you make a conscious effort to remain nonjudgmental and ask questions rather than tell your smoker what to do, chances are good he'll be willing to share with you.

Be sure to listen to your smoker. You may discover what's really preventing her from quitting. Once you know, you'll be able to help her focus on a solution. But no matter how brilliant you think your ideas are, don't present them to your smoker as a formula for change. Instead, ask, "What will help you quit?" Let her come up with her own answers. People resist ideas that aren't their own. And if quitting isn't your smoker's own idea, it's destined to fail.

❧ Chapter Eight ❧

STEP 5: OVERCOME THE FEAR
OF FAILURE
Contemplative Stage

Once your smoker begins to talk about quitting, it's vitally important to build his confidence. Most smokers suffer from low self-esteem. It's one of the reasons many of them started smoking in the first place. If they didn't have low self-esteem before they started, they certainly suffer from it afterward. Smokers have become the ultimate social pariahs. Most of society views them as behaving in a totally self-indulgent manner by continuing to smoke in spite of overwhelming evidence against it. People who don't smoke resent having to pay increased health insurance premiums and higher taxes for public health programs because of those who do. Most people, of course, have no idea how great is the desperation of smokers who really want to quit but because of physiological and psychological addiction don't believe they can.

To make matters worse, it's possible that the smoker you care about has tried to quit. Maybe more than once. Maybe even many times. Every single time she fell off the tobacco wagon, she was probably overwhelmed by a sense of failure so profound she was ashamed to admit it to anyone for a long time. Even now, years after I quit smoking, I still dream that I've started again. The disappointment is so terrible that I often wake with tears in my eyes. Starting to smoke again after letting the world know you've quit (and receiving the world's congratulations) is one of the worst feelings I've ever known. It always left my self-worth in tatters, and it's one more reason why smokers who really want to quit often don't. They're afraid of failing again. They just can't take the damage to their self-esteem when they try and fail to quit once more.

Most people try and fail many times before they quit for life. I've personally never met anyone who succeeded on the first try. The great American humorist Mark Twain summed it up when he said, "I can quit smoking anytime I want to. I've quit a thousand times!" The average smoker makes about ten quit attempts before becoming a long-term quitter. I used to think I was unique for having tried and failed to quit so many times. What a relief it was to discover that I was actually pretty close to average.

Among the maternal maxims I used with my son while he was growing up was "Our greatest glory lies not in never falling but in rising each time we fall." Like many kids, he was often reluctant to try new things for fear of appearing foolish if he failed. But I always told him that the only real failure was the failure to try. According to Jack Canfield, speaker, trainer, consultant, and author of numerous books about self-esteem, most millionaires file bankruptcy several times before they achieve financial success. A person who will not risk failure will probably never be successful.

One of the most important lessons in life is that we learn from our mistakes. Every time I tried and failed to quit smoking, I learned something that helped me stay away from cigarettes a little longer the next time. I analyzed each pit I fell into until I became so surefooted that I didn't fall anymore. I believe that every time a smoker tries and fails to quit, it's cause for celebration. It means he is that much closer to ultimate success. The secret is not to let repeated failures keep your smoker from trying again.

A lack of self-esteem may be one reason your smoker is reluctant to quit. She may have been led to believe that smoking gives her power, control, independence, personal style, or something else she feels is lacking. By helping her believe in herself and by augmenting her ability to feel powerful and in control, you greatly enhance her ability to quit.

Positive self-esteem usually comes from within. But poor self-esteem often results from being repeatedly torn down by others. This frequently occurs in childhood, when we develop our sense of ourselves. But poor self-esteem developed in childhood can be overcome by learning to "reparent" ourselves as adults. Doing this requires us to get in touch with the childlike part of ourselves and, as responsible adults, practice the techniques of building positive self-esteem. Following are a few of the methods experts recommend to build a child's self-esteem. But let's substitute the word *smoker* for *child* and see if it strikes any chords:

- Accept your smoker for who he is—and help him do the same.
- Allow your smoker to make her own choices.
- Avoid criticizing your smoker.
- Emphasize the positive things about your smoker and praise the positive things he does.
- Be supportive of your smoker's goals.

You can do—and avoid doing—much more to help your smoker develop self-confidence and self-respect. For example:

- When you are tempted to declare how wrong your smoker is, you can ask her to clarify or to explain what she is thinking or feeling. People tend to express themselves more freely if they don't feel the threat of a judge's sentence.
- When a nagging session threatens to erupt, try humor. Nagging destroys communication. Humor can salvage it.
- When emotional stress is evident, talk about the problem later. Strong emotion makes productive dialogue impossible. Let the emotion subside before tackling the problem.

One way to check on people's self-esteem is to observe how they handle failure. If, for example, they try to quit smoking but start up again after a few weeks or months, they may look at it as a chance to figure out what they did wrong. Or they may blame stress, circumstances, or their own innate weakness (that is, something over which they have no control). People with strong self-esteem believe their success is based on what they do. It comes from inside. People with low self-esteem often pin their success (or lack of success) on their failure or simply fate.

The reaction of the people who care for smokers is essential. Smokers need to know that nobody is perfect and nobody expects them to be. You may yearn for them to quit smoking, but it isn't the end of the world if they fail at one attempt. Remember, they can always try again. Your job is to convince them to keep trying.

To help build self-esteem in your smoker, you can say things like:

- Great job!
- You're the expert on this . . .
- What do you think?
- I'm really proud of you.
- Thank you.

You can also avoid saying things like:

- That's ridiculous!
- You wouldn't understand.
- Let me do it, you'll only get it wrong.
- Will you ever learn?
- Can't you do anything right?
- If I were you, this is the way I'd do it.

Remember the story *The Little Engine That Could*? Your job is to keep whispering, "I think you can, I think you can!" into your smoker's ear until he begins to whisper back, "I know I can, I know I can!" Building confidence and self-esteem is part of that effort. Once your smoker has the confidence to overcome his fear of failure, then and only then will he become a successful quitter.

○ Chapter Nine ◎

STEP 6: FOCUS ON THE PRESENT
Preparation Stage

The day has arrived. Your smoker has said she's either thinking about quitting or is ready to quit. First of all, hallelujah! But resist the urge to remind her of all the health benefits of quitting. Once she quits she will be glad she no longer has to worry about the dangers of smoking. But reminding her prematurely of what could happen if she *doesn't* quit may trigger denial.

Instead, keep your focus on the present. Congratulate him for his decision. Offer your support and encouragement. Remind your smoker how much better life will be *right now* without the inconvenience and expense of tobacco. Then clam up and wait for your smoker to make the next move. I know this is difficult, but if you say too much, you run the risk of descending into nagging. Always remember, it's up to the smoker to do the heavy lifting. If you try to force the issue, you could propel him backward into defiance.

It's an odd quirk that most smokers have, but the health consequences of smoking rarely factor into their decision to quit. Once they actually *do* quit, well, then they're thrilled they no longer have to worry about all those scary-sounding diseases. But until then, it's just something they *might* get someday in the far-distant future. Most smokers are in denial about the future. They rarely consider what might happen tomorrow until the addict that lives within them loses some of its power. What works best with most smokers is telling them how much better their lives can be in the present without the burden of cigarettes.

This inability to consider the future is hard for many non-smokers to understand. But I've seen proof of it. I can't count the times I've heard smokers say stress is the reason they continue to smoke, but they sparkle like Christmas trees when I tell them they'll handle stress much better once the nicotine is out of their system. "Really?" they'll say. "I never knew that!" Stress is something all smokers know about. It's part of their present. Yet if I utter a word about the million and one diseases they're likely to develop sometime in the future if they *don't* quit, their eyes glaze over, they shift from one foot to another, and they tune out. I've said something they don't want to hear. I've mentioned the future, and the future is something they've had a lot of practice not thinking about.

The present is where it's at for most smokers, but once they start thinking seriously about quitting, the future may stretch ahead of them bleakly. For years, if not most of smokers' lives, cigarettes have been their friend and constant companion. How will they manage everyday situations without cigarettes? How in the world can they possibly cope with any type of crisis? The fact is, they *can* manage without cigarettes, probably much better than they ever did *with* them. But until smokers experience those benefits for themselves, they often prefer to exist in their own twilight world where myths rule and truth is stranger than fiction. Change is frightening for most people, even when it's a change for the better. They know what life was like as a smoker. It may have had its drawbacks, but at least it was familiar. A future as a nonsmoker, however, is *terra incognita*. It's new territory, a strange new world, and more than a little terrifying.

After uttering those magic words—"I want to quit smoking"—your smoker may still display ambivalence. Even as smokers go about preparing to quit, some continue to defend their right to smoke based on myths that the tobacco industry and the addict who lives within them have convinced them to believe. These smokers are still headed in the right direction, but they may feel nervous or uncertain about their ability to handle withdrawal or develop new coping skills. This is your chance to reassure such smokers of your confidence in them and, as long as you're at it, debunk some of the myths about tobacco.

So pervasive are these myths that you may have believed some of them yourself. Here are just a few. See how many you thought were true.

Myth #1: Smoking calms me down when I'm nervous or anxious.

Quite the opposite. A report in the *American Journal of Psychiatry* described a study in England that found no evidence of increased anxiety in patients who gave up smoking. In fact, they found *a significant decrease in anxiety* beginning in the first nicotine-free week. These results led researchers to conclude that smoking leads to increased anxiety and that giving up smoking improves the situation.[1]

Many smokers who try to quit note increased anxiety as part of nicotine withdrawal. The anxiety that smokers experience when they quit is part of their withdrawal. But here's an important distinction: *Smoking does not relieve stress.* Smoking actually *increases* stress because every twenty to thirty minutes the smoker's brain signals the need for more nicotine. This triggers withdrawal, which causes stress, which leads to another cigarette to relieve the stress of withdrawal. The cycle repeats itself over and over until nicotine is completely flushed out of the smoker's system.

Once she has rid her body of nicotine, your smoker will probably feel less anxious. She'll find it easier to deal with stress. The good news is that it only takes about three to five days to rid the body of nicotine. (It goes faster if you force fluids—more about that later.) So using stress as an excuse to avoid quitting isn't really valid. Most smokers deal with stress better once they quit.

Myth #2: Smoking picks me up when I'm down and makes the good times better.

Although it's still a myth, there is actually a chemical basis for this illusion. (For details, read **Step 13: Consider the Link between Smoking and Depression.**) Because I suffered from depression, I used this argument a lot. When people nagged me about smoking,

I would say, "Smoking is my only vice. It's the only thing I do for myself." I realized how silly this sounded when a friend responded with, "So sucking a quart of tar into your lungs every day is the best thing you can think of to do for yourself?" I mean, seriously, how pathetic is that?

I'm proud to say that I've since learned better ways of being nice to myself. These days when I need a pick-me-up, I call a friend, get a massage, take a walk, soak in a hot tub, listen to my favorite CD, or buy myself some flowers. Now that I'm not spending so much money on cigarettes, I can afford little luxuries. Each of these treats is not only much more pleasant than smoking, but also the effects last a lot longer.

Myth #3: Smoking gives me energy.

This is nonsense! One of the deceptive things about nicotine is that it acts as both a stimulant and a depressant. The immediate effect is stimulating—that's the rush people feel after smoking. But soon, the depressant takes over, causing the smoker to feel sluggish. This creates a craving for the lift provided by the stimulant. This is followed by the typical down feeling that leads to another urge for a cigarette. And so it goes.

Among the immediate effects of quitting are feelings of fatigue and listlessness. Part of this is the body's attempt to heal itself from the damage caused by cigarettes. It's the same feeling you have when you're recovering from a cold or the flu. But this feeling disappears with time. Eventually ex-smokers have much more energy than they ever had when they smoked. They will be amazed at how animated and lively they feel. A temporary loss of energy is a small price to pay for the renewed vitality they'll experience once those harmful drugs are out of their system.

Myth #4: Alcohol and other drugs are more deadly than smoking.

Let's take a look at the way the numbers add up:

Cause of Death	Deaths per Year
Smoking	434,000[2]
Secondhand smoke (passive smoking)	53,000[3]
Alcohol (including drunk driving)	125,000[4]
Car accidents	47,000[5]
Suicide	31,000[6]
AIDS	23,000[7]
Homicide	22,000[8]
Fires	4,000[9]
Cocaine and crack	3,300[10]
Heroin and morphine	2,400[11]

I often hear parents and educators express concern over the serious drugs that affect young people while virtually ignoring the billowing clouds of smoke that hover over many school yards and school bus stops. Take another look at those numbers. Tobacco kills nearly half a million Americans each year, more than all the illegal drugs, alcohol, AIDS, homicide, suicide, car accidents, and fires combined. One out of three kids who starts smoking today will die prematurely and perhaps horribly from a tobacco addiction. How much more serious can a drug get?

Myth #5: If I quit smoking, I'll get fat.

Not all quitters gain weight. Some actually lose weight because of increased exercise and better nutrition. Also, evidence suggests that smokers tend to carry more weight around the abdomen. This puts them at an increased risk for diabetes and heart disease. This is due to the changes smoking causes in the body's hormonal balance.[12] If your smoker has a problem with abdominal fat, a real trouble spot for some people, quitting smoking may actually make it easier to lose that spare tire.

We live in a very weight-conscious society. People judge obesity even more harshly than addictive behavior like smoking. Fear of gaining weight is one of the top reasons smokers cite for not giving up cigarettes. But anyone who has mastered nicotine dependency can easily lose the six to twelve pounds gained by the average quitter. I gained a little weight when I first quit smoking. But thanks to an improved diet and daily exercise, I'm now in better shape than I was in high school. Believe me, compared to quitting smoking, losing weight is a snap.

Myth #6: I've quit so many times already, I'm destined to keep smoking for the rest of my life.

After twelve quit attempts, I'm proof that this myth is precisely that. Most ex-smokers cycle through the quitting process many times before becoming long-term quitters. At least one-third of smokers who stay off cigarettes for one or more years may eventually relapse. However, relapse becomes less likely as ex-smokers stay off cigarettes for longer periods of time. And every single time they quit makes it that much more likely that the next attempt will be the one that will keep them off cigarettes for life.

Myth #7: I've been smoking so long the damage is already done. I might as well keep smoking until it kills me.

It's rarely too late to quit. According to a study by the National Cancer Institute, even lung cancer survivors who kick the habit are less likely to develop a second cancer than those who continue to smoke.[13]

True, the lung cancer survival rates are pretty dismal. Emphysema is another disease caused by smoking whose effects can't be reversed. But for those who quit, survival rates are at the higher end of the range.

If the smoker you care about hasn't yet developed a disease such as lung cancer or emphysema, his quality of life can be greatly enhanced by quitting now. Just minutes after quitting, the body begins a series of healing changes that go on for years.[14] Unless permanent damage has already occurred, most of the harmful effects of smoking can actually be reversed. So let the smoker you care about know that it's never too late.

Myth #8: I smoke light cigarettes, which are safer than the old, stronger brands.

There is no such thing as a safe cigarette. In fact, some research indicates that light cigarettes promote cancers that are harder to find and more difficult to cure than those caused by the old-fashioned, "dangerous" brands.

Smokers of filtered, low-nicotine cigarettes tend to inhale more deeply to get the same amount of nicotine. This draws the smoke deeper into the lungs and keeps it there longer. Also, the next time you get a chance, take a look at the filters on those light cigarettes. You will likely find tiny holes punched into the filter, which are supposed to release some of the tar and other harmful ingredients in cigarette smoke before it is inhaled. However, because they're usually placed at the tip of the cigarette where smokers' lips or fingers cover them at every puff, the purpose is utterly defeated.

Earlier generations of smokers tended to have squamous cell, or small cell, lung cancers. These cancers are usually found in the lining of the larger air tubes within the pulmonary system. In recent years, we've seen an increase in lung cancers of the small air sacs and tubes deep in the lungs, which many scientists attribute to the use of filter-tipped cigarettes with milder tobacco.[15] Considering that death rates from these types of cancers are even higher than squamous cell lung cancers (whose survival rates aren't exactly rosy), light cigarettes don't appear to be much of a bargain in the health sweepstakes.

Myth #9: Only old people die of tobacco-related diseases. I'll quit before it happens to me.

We are seeing an alarming increase in lung cancer and emphysema among smokers and former smokers in their forties, thirties, and even younger. Part of this is due to the age many of them started smoking. People who start smoking in their early teens introduce dangerous environmental toxins (cigarette smoke) into their systems at a time when their bodies are going through the process of rapid cell division known as puberty. The damage this causes can be irreversible. Cancer may not show up for ten, twenty, even thirty years later. Meanwhile, these people are like walking time bombs.[16]

The threat of premature death exists with other forms of tobacco as well. Consider the case of Sean Marsee, a young Oklahoma athlete who started chewing tobacco when he was twelve years old. At eighteen, Sean was diagnosed with an advanced oral cancer that rapidly spread throughout his body. He underwent radical surgery, including the removal of his jaw, his tongue, and the glands in his neck, all to no avail. The young man died a year later, shortly after his high school graduation. He'd been using spit tobacco for just six years, and he paid a heavy price for it. So did his heartbroken family.

The smoker you care about may come up with other myths not listed here. But no matter what arguments he uses, keep in mind that there's not a single valid reason to continue smoking, but there are many good reasons to quit. By helping to debunk some of these myths, your smoker may soon come to share this belief.

☙ Chapter Ten ❧

STEP 7: EXPLORE STOP-SMOKING TREATMENTS
Preparation Stage

Once your smoker reaches the preparation stage, the main question on his mind will likely be "How?" Unless he is prepared to listen to a lot of unsolicited advice, he probably shouldn't ask this question out loud in public places. Everyone who has ever quit smoking, along with a few who have never smoked a cigarette in their lives, all seem to know the one, absolutely sure way to go about it.

Smokers who are ready to quit may be confused by the wide variety of stop-smoking methods available. Some people swear by pills and potions while others tough it out by going cold turkey. Some like a nicotine patch. Others prefer diet and exercise. Some like acupuncture or meditation. I even knew one ex-smoker who vowed that a pinkie ring in the shape of a no-smoking sign had done the trick for him.

I don't believe there is a single method for quitting smoking that is right for everyone. Smokers, like all of us, are individuals. What works for one person may not work for another. Every method has its share of risks and drawbacks. Nevertheless, I've yet to hear of any stop-smoking risk that equals the risks of smoking.

Following are descriptions of a few of the stop-smoking treatments available. If your smoker is discouraged about quitting because she's tried one, two, or even three therapies that didn't work, encourage her to keep trying. Keep in mind that I tried a dozen different treatments before I found one that helped me quit for life. By educating yourself about these treatments, you can help your smoker find one that works.

Behavior Modification Programs

Behavior modification is the traditional way to quit smoking. Organizations such as the American Cancer Society, public health clinics, community hospitals, and chemical dependency treatment centers offer such programs. Some employers now offer these programs as part of their employee benefits package.

This concept works on the idea that smokers can change their behavior with information and strategies to help them direct their own efforts to quit. One advantage these programs offer is peer support. Others who are going through the same thing make quitters feel less isolated and enable them to compare notes and experiences.

Some states now offer individual stop-smoking counseling through telephone "quit line" services. Some private counselors also offer this type of individualized support. The advantages include privacy and the opportunity to personalize the quitting plan to the needs of the individual. The disadvantages include cost (private counseling for smoking cessation can be expensive, and it's generally not covered by insurance, though telephone quit line services are free to residents of some states) and little to no opportunity to share experiences with other quitters.

Some type of cessation counseling or classes is highly recommended for anyone attempting to quit smoking. Studies have shown that adding Zyban and/or nicotine replacement therapy (NRT) to an effective behavior modification program can greatly increase a smoker's chances of quitting successfully.[1]

Behavior modification programs and counselors often recommend one or more of the following approaches:

- *Cold turkey* is an abrupt cessation from smoking. If your smoker regularly smokes one pack of cigarettes a day, with the cold turkey method, he will smoke a pack one day but no cigarettes the next day and thereafter.

- *Tapering* is a gradual method of quitting. This method requires the smoker to count the number of cigarettes she smokes per day and then to smoke fewer cigarettes each day. For example, a smoker might try to reduce the number of cigarettes she smokes by five cigarettes a day for six days, at which point she will quit. Cutting down by just one or two cigarettes a day is generally not advisable unless the individual is already a light smoker. Also, no gradual method of quitting should be extended for longer than a week. Anything more than that can be a way of avoiding quitting.

- *Postponing* is another gradual method. The smoker postpones the time when he starts smoking by a certain number of hours each day. Once he begins smoking, he doesn't have to count cigarettes or worry about reducing the number. What may happen is that more cigarettes will be smoked later in the day to get the nicotine back up to target levels. Nevertheless, this can be an effective method of disassociating smoking with certain behaviors at certain times of day (for example, smoking a cigarette with a morning cup of coffee).

- *Nicotine fading* is a method in which smokers switch to cigarettes with less tar and nicotine. The theory is that quitting will be easier if the smoker lowers her body's levels of nicotine. Smokers may try to compensate by inhaling more deeply or smoking more cigarettes.

- *Setting a quit date* is highly recommended by most behavior modification programs. I also recommend this. Quitting is often easier if the smoker chooses a day or days likely to be relatively low in stress. For example, it would be a bad idea to quit smoking on the first day of a new job, the day a divorce becomes final, or the week the in-laws are coming for a visit. Some people find it easier to quit during the week when work and other responsibilities keep mind, hands, and body occupied. Others prefer to quit over a weekend when they can pamper themselves.

It's really up to the individual, but encourage your smoker to set a quit date and then urge him to stick with it. This is a contract he makes with himself, but if you can get him to tell you when he plans to put this contract into effect, he may feel more of an obligation to honor it.

Non-Nicotine Replacement Therapy

Zyban, also known as Wellbutrin, or its generic name, bupropion, is an antidepressant drug that can greatly increase a smoker's chances of quitting, especially when combined with behavior modification therapy (stop-smoking classes or counseling). Based on most of the studies I've seen, Zyban is the single best tool currently available for helping smokers quit.

Unfortunately, not everyone can take this drug. People with seizure disorders (such as epilepsy), people who are already taking Wellbutrin or other medicines containing bupropion for other medical conditions, those who now have or have had an eating disorder, and individuals who are currently taking or have recently taken a monoamine oxidase inhibitor (MAOI) should not take Zyban to help quit smoking. Also, Zyban is not recommended for pregnant women or women who are breast-feeding.

Zyban is the only nicotine-free medication approved by the U.S. Food and Drug Administration (FDA) for quitting smoking. Though it is an antidepressant, it appears to be effective in helping smokers quit, even those who don't show typical symptoms of clinical depression. Other drugs have shown promise in stop-smoking trials, including the well-known antidepressant Prozac. These drugs, however, target different brain chemicals and have not been specifically approved for use in stop-smoking programs.

Another advantage of Zyban is that it appears to prevent quitters from gaining as much weight as those who quit smoking using other methods. People taking Zyban put on an average of just three to four pounds, compared with six to twelve pounds for successful quitters who did not take Zyban. Some Zyban users even report a slight weight loss.

Unlike other antidepressants, Zyban does not cause a loss of sex drive. In fact, some early studies suggest that Zyban may increase libido in women and may enhance sexual pleasure in both genders.

Zyban can be prescribed only by a physician. Advise your smoker to check with her doctor to see if she is a candidate for this drug. (Also, be sure to read **Step 13: Consider the Link between Smoking and Depression.**)

Nicotine Replacement Therapy

Using nicotine substitutes such as the patch or nicotine gum can also increase your smoker's chances of quitting successfully. Some studies have shown that NRT, by itself, is only about half as effective as Zyban alone. However, nicotine replacement therapy in conjunction with Zyban and stop-smoking classes or counseling have shown the most promising long-term quit rates I've seen. Some people, of course, cannot use Zyban. For these individuals, nicotine replacement products are an alternative.

I am always amazed when smokers tell me they're reluctant to try Zyban or nicotine replacement products because of the so-called risks. Compared to smoking, the risk of using Zyban or nicotine replacement therapy is small. A study by the American Lung Association showed that an astonishing number of people believe the nicotine in cigarettes is what causes cancer. Nicotine is highly addictive. In uncontrolled dosages, it can also be toxic, but it's the tar and the many other harmful chemicals in cigarette smoke that cause cancer, not the nicotine. In fact, studies with long-term users of nicotine gum have shown no harmful effects.

Nicotine does, however, cause elevated blood pressure even in controlled doses. Therefore, nicotine replacement therapy is not recommended for people with heart problems or history of stroke. It's also not recommended for pregnant or nursing women.

There are many more NRT options available now than when I used the patch to quit smoking. Following are a few of the choices:

Nicotine patches deliver a measured dose of nicotine through the skin. As nicotine doses are lowered over a period of time, the smoker is weaned from nicotine. Nicotine patches are now available without a prescription, but they do not work for everyone. Your smoker should also be aware that the nicotine patch doesn't work the way cigarettes do. For one thing, it takes about an hour for nicotine delivered transdermally (through the skin) to reach the brain, whereas inhaled smoke delivers nicotine to the brain within seconds. Nicotine patches deliver a constant, steady dose of nicotine into the bloodstream, while cigarette smokers experience more of a rise and fall of nicotine levels. Smokers accustomed to a periodic spike of nicotine often have a hard time adjusting to the steadier levels the patch provides.

Pregnant women, nursing mothers, and people with certain health conditions who take other prescription drugs or who are under a doctor's care should talk with their physicians about the potential risks of nicotine patches and weigh these against the known risks of continuing to smoke. A doctor's advice is always the best guide when dealing with concerns about the patch.

Patch users should never, ever smoke or use other nicotine-containing products while on the patch. Doing so could result in nicotine poisoning and may cause a dangerous elevation in blood pressure.

Side effects of the patch include skin irritation, rapid pulse, dizziness, nausea, vomiting, muscle aches and stiffness, headaches, and vivid, bizarre dreams. Sometimes switching to a different brand helps solve the problem.

Nicotine gum allows controlled doses of nicotine to be absorbed through the mucous membranes of the mouth. It takes about ten minutes for nicotine absorbed this way to reach the brain. Nicotine gum has the advantage of allowing smokers greater control over nicotine doses. Like the patch, it's available without a prescription. It comes in 2-mg and 4-mg strengths.

Nicotine gum should not be used like chewing gum. Users chew a piece until it softens and creates a tingling or peppery sensation inside the mouth. The gum is then "parked" against the cheek until the tingling fades. Chewing is then resumed until the tingling returns; the gum is then parked, then chewed, and so on. Food and drink can affect the way nicotine is absorbed, so food and beverages should be avoided for at least fifteen minutes before and after using the gum.

Nicotine gum, like the patch, should always be carefully discarded and should be kept out of the reach of children and pets. As with the patch, *nicotine gum users should never smoke or use other nicotine-containing products while using nicotine gum.*

Side effects of nicotine gum include mouth sores, rapid pulse, nausea, and headaches. Be aware that some people become addicted to nicotine gum (about 10 percent of users) and find it difficult to give up.

Nicotine nasal spray delivers nicotine through the nose so that less nicotine is absorbed into the brain than from cigarettes. Unlike the patch or nicotine gum, it provides instant relief from cravings by delivering nicotine into the bloodstream very quickly. Nicotine nasal spray is available only with a prescription.

The most common side effects include nasal irritation, runny nose, watery eyes, sneezing, throat irritation, and coughing. People with allergies, asthma, nasal polyps, or sinus trouble may want to use another form of nicotine replacement therapy.

Nicotine inhalers are cigarette-like devices that allow the user to inhale nicotine just as they would with a cigarette but without the harmful effects of tar and other poisonous gases in cigarette smoke. Like the nasal spray, the nicotine inhaler is available only with a doctor's prescription. Side effects may include coughing and throat irritation.

Other Stop-Smoking Methods

Hypnosis seems to work for some people, though there is no scientific proof of its effectiveness. If your smoker decides to try hypnosis, warn him to be on guard: Anyone can claim to be a hypnotist. Licensing is not required. I went to a licensed hypnotist during one of my quit attempts, but it didn't work for me. On the other hand, I may not have been a good subject for hypnosis.

Acupuncture is something else I tried that seemed to work for a little while, though I eventually went back to smoking. Scientific evidence in support of this method is scanty, but Western medicine has always tended to view Eastern methods, such as acupuncture, with suspicion. Acupuncture may be an effective way of reducing stress or tension while going through withdrawal. I recently underwent acupuncture treatment for a back injury, which provided more relief than any of the traditional therapies I had tried, so I'm willing to concede that it may also be an effective piece of a stop-smoking plan. For a list of physician acupuncturists in your area, contact the American Academy of Medical Acupuncture (AAMA). (See the **Resource List** at the end of this book.)

Disposable filters that reduce tar and nicotine are generally considered ineffective. These are often sold in drugstores alongside other over-the-counter medications, though some stores place them near the cigarette displays. Some studies show that smokers who use these filters actually smoke more. This was another method I tried and gave up when my jaw began to ache from inhaling hard enough to feel like I was smoking. If anything, the filters increased my desire to smoke.

Smoking deterrents are over-the-counter drugs that are supposed to alter the taste of tobacco, reduce cravings, alleviate tension, and flush nicotine out of the body. *Stop-smoking diets* also claim to diminish nicotine cravings. Neither of these methods have demonstrated any scientific evidence of effectiveness.

Some people claim that *herbal remedies* are helpful in quitting smoking. Although there is no scientific basis for these claims, some herbs may provide a relaxant or soothing effect. I drank a lot of herbal tea when I quit smoking, which helped flush the nicotine out of my system and calmed jangled nerves when cravings hit.

Beware, however, that herbal remedies are not approved by the FDA, which means doses and quality are not regulated. In addition, some herbs may interfere with or counteract prescribed medication. Your smoker needs to inform her physician of any herbal remedies she's considering in order to avoid potentially harmful interactions.

If the smoker you care about wants to quit cold turkey, more power to him. As for me, I think cold turkey tastes great in a sandwich or a salad, but it can be a tough way to quit smoking. I once heard an addiction specialist testify that the people who *can* quit smoking cold turkey have, for the most part, already done so, but the ones who are still smoking probably need help. If your smoker needs or wants help to quit, encourage him to get it. Quitting smoking is hard enough without tossing performance standards into the mix.

I also want to add a few words of caution about some stop-smoking treatments. When I first went to work for the American Cancer Society, hardly a week would go by that I didn't receive a call from someone claiming to have discovered a foolproof way to help people quit smoking. Most of the time I simply explained that we did not promote commercial products, but every once in a while I agreed to give the callers a little feedback. The products they sent me ranged from the ridiculous to the sublime, but all had one thing in common: Somebody was trying to make a lot of money.

Nearly all stop-smoking products or services are developed by people who understand that most smokers are desperate to quit and will pay almost anything to break their addiction. Many of these products don't work, but even those that do are frequently motivated more by profit than altruism. As long as a week's supply of cigarettes costs $25 to $30 while a box of nicotine patches or gum costs anywhere from $60 to $75, there will be many smokers who continue to smoke because they can't afford to quit.

Insurance companies and health maintenance organizations (HMOs) are another pet peeve of mine. Granted, there are excellent stop-smoking clinics offered by managed care organizations, but most third-party providers, who often cover the cost of alcohol and drug rehabilitation, will not pay for smoking cessation therapies, including those with proven track records.

Considering what these companies might save by helping people quit before the ravages of lung cancer, emphysema, and heart disease eat away their profits, it simply makes good financial sense for insurers and managed care providers to contribute to the cost of smoking cessation treatment. As of this writing, however, few of them do. I'm hoping this will change as more providers realize how much sense it makes, from both a financial and humanitarian perspective.

◌ Chapter Eleven ◌

STEP 8: GET PHYSICAL
Preparation/Action Stage

You won't catch many Olympic athletes smoking. But you don't have to be in training for a gold medal to realize that an active lifestyle, more often than not, is associated with other healthy behavior. More than one smoker has made the decision to quit after starting a new exercise program and discovering that cigarettes have affected her stamina as well as her lung capacity.

The association between exercise and healthy living is sometimes called "the granola effect." This is what happens when one healthy behavior leads to another. By encouraging your smoker to begin an exercise program as part of his stop-smoking effort, you can go a long way toward helping him quit and stay quit.

Smokers who are physically active have a lower risk of dying of heart attack or stroke. Even for smokers who don't quit or quitters who relapse, exercise gives them a distinct edge over inactive smokers when it comes to cardiovascular health. Keep in mind, however, that sedentary nonsmokers have the advantage over physically active smokers. The group with the lowest risk of heart attack or stroke are physically active nonsmokers.[1] This, of course, is the group you want your smoker to join.

Exercise has many advantages for smokers who are trying to quit. For one thing, it speeds up metabolism, thereby replacing the metabolic boost provided by nicotine. It also builds muscle, strength, and stamina, and is a vital factor in weight control, a source of concern for many smokers. Those who exercise as part of a stop-smoking program gain only half the weight gained by quitters who don't exercise.

Exercise is an important factor in helping your smoker stay quit. Quitters who exercise have a lower relapse rate than those who don't exercise.[2] From a purely practical perspective, it's difficult to exercise and smoke at the same time. Smoking is not allowed in a gym, nor is it feasible to smoke while jogging, swimming, or working out on a treadmill. Exercise is also a great way to regenerate a body that has been abused by cigarettes.

Vigorous exercise also produces endorphins, "feel-good" chemicals that create a mood-enhancing, energy-stimulating high. But unlike the artificial high provided by cigarettes, the energy burst produced by exercise lasts for hours and doesn't result in down feelings after the effects wear off.

Many people report increases in stress and anxiety immediately after they give up cigarettes. Exercise gives ex-smokers alternative ways of dealing with stress. It can also increase their sense of mastery and control by helping them realize they really *can* cope with stress without resorting to cigarettes or some other potentially harmful, mood-altering drug such as alcohol.

I used to think I didn't have the time or energy for exercise. But once I became convinced of its benefits, I started getting up an hour earlier in the morning to make time for a daily workout. Not only did I enjoy the advantages of a firmer body and better resistance to colds and flu, but exercise gave me a burst of energy that lasted all day long, far more than if I had spent that extra hour in bed. I still have to fight a natural desire to roll over and go back to sleep when the alarm rings before dawn, but once I'm actually up and about, I'm always glad I didn't give in. The benefits of exercise far exceed any so-called benefits I used to get from the cigarette I once had with my morning coffee. Exercise has become part of my daily routine. I would no more skip it now than I would skip brushing my teeth or taking a shower.

One way to get your smoker to start exercising is to exercise with her. People who exercise with a partner or a group tend to enjoy it more and stick with it longer. Remember, you don't have to train for a marathon to be physically active. Your daily exercise can be as simple as a brisk walk. Find something you both enjoy doing and do it together. Take bicycle rides, go swimming, bowling, or dancing, play golf, tennis, racquetball, or badminton, or sign up for an aerobics class together. Even gardening provides physical benefits.

It's best to vary your activities to avoid boredom. It doesn't matter what you do so long as it involves some form of physical activity and you do it on a regular basis. The important thing is to stick with it and make it part of your daily routine. Just get the body moving. That, all by itself, is likely to be a big change in your smoker's routine.

It's amazing how much time smokers spend sitting and smoking. Having a cigarette is often an excuse for some people to take a break. Somehow, it seems less like goofing off if you can smoke a cigarette instead of sitting and relaxing. Smoking can also be a great excuse to avoid physical activity. Nature, however, abhors a vacuum. So in the absence of cigarettes, your ex-smoker will need some other activity to take their place. That's why this is such a great time for your ex-smoker to begin an exercise routine. Instead of having a cigarette, he can do simple stretching exercises, take a walk around the block, practice deep breathing—anything, so long as it fills the void left by cigarettes.

Deep breathing, by the way, is a great cigarette substitute. In the act of smoking a cigarette, smokers are accustomed to inhaling or breathing deeply. Unfortunately, what they get with each of these deep breaths is a lot of tar and nicotine instead of the oxygen their bodies crave. The good news is that they can get something close to the same satisfaction by breathing pure, fresh air. Whenever an urge to smoke hits, encourage your ex-smoker to breathe in through her nose, feeling the air push all the way to the bottom of her diaphragm. Then exhale through the mouth until all the air is forced out of the lungs. She should repeat this process several times or until the urge to smoke passes. And keep reminding her that it *will* pass. That's something most ex-smokers have a hard time believing at first. Most cravings are limited to just a minute or two. So long as ex-smokers can distract themselves with some activity other than smoking, nicotine cravings will gradually subside until they finally lose the power to control.

It's always a good idea for your ex-smoker to check with a doctor before starting any exercise program, especially if he was used to smoking more than a pack a day. For very heavy smokers, vigorous exercise may create too much of a strain on the heart. It's best for him to start slowly. He can begin with just ten minutes a day. Eventually, he can work his way up to at least thirty minutes of regular, sustained activity. Your ex-smoker will find this enormously helpful in the effort to quit smoking. If you join him, you'll receive the benefits, too!

Changes in activity patterns can make a huge difference in your ex-smoker's success or failure in conquering addiction. But exercise should never be regarded as a substitute for quitting. Even the most ideal exercise program cannot make up for the tremendous damage smokers do to their bodies with cigarettes, but greater mindfulness of their overall health can nudge smokers out of denial while focusing more attention on physical fitness. At the least, exercise will make smokers feel better about themselves and their bodies. Once they do, they may just decide to go the whole way.

ꙮ Chapter Twelve ꙮ

STEP 9: FOOD FOR THOUGHT
Preparation/Action Stage

One reason it's so hard to quit smoking is because of the apparently positive ways nicotine affects the body. Nicotine causes the metabolism to work faster. It also causes an increase in blood sugar, which gives smokers a brief, temporary burst of energy. This is the high or stimulant effect many smokers experience when they smoke. But it's usually followed fifteen to twenty minutes later by a drop in blood sugar. This creates a low or depressant effect that causes smokers to crave cigarettes to get the high feeling again.

When smokers are deprived of nicotine for long periods of time (such as when they try to quit), the drop in blood sugar creates a false impression of hunger, particularly cravings for something sweet. These cravings, combined with a smoker's strongly reinforced habit of constantly putting something in the mouth, is the reason many smokers pig out when they quit smoking.[1]

Fortunately, there are ways of creating the same highs, or positive effects, without the lows, or negative effects, that lead to the desire to smoke. Accomplishing this requires changes in diet.

Five a Day Makes the Marlboro Man Go Away

The diets of most smokers are lower in nutrition than the average person's. One reason for this is denial. After all, if smokers are immune to the dangers of cigarettes, why would sugar or choles-terol have any power to harm them? Another reason smokers have a worse diet is that the subtle flavors of fruits and vegetables are lost on most of them. They crave strong flavors and rich spices, which is all their smoke-deadened taste buds can discern.

Smokers need large amounts of vitamins A and C, which are found primarily in fruits and vegetables. Foods rich in vitamin A can help prevent lung cancer. Vitamin C helps prevent cancers of the mouth and throat. The American Cancer Society recommends a minimum of five servings a day of fruits and vegetables to help prevent cancer, but smokers tend to eat less than this even though they need these nutrients so much more.[2]

In addition to containing vitamins, fruits and vegetables contain water, fiber, and antioxidant minerals that rid the body of harmful elements, including some of the poisons in cigarettes. Not even bushels of carrots or carloads of strawberries can counter all the damage smoking causes, but over time eating more fruits and vege-tables certainly helps the process. Because most plant-based foods are filling and relatively low in calories, they also help prevent weight gain.

You may be thinking: "If the smoker I care about quits, why should we worry about cancer?" It's true that quitting greatly re-duces the risk of cancer, but there's no way of knowing how much cell damage may have occurred during all those years of inhaling poisons on a daily basis. Cancers have been known to show up years, even decades, after smoking that last cigarette. Eating a diet rich in cancer-preventing vitamins may provide a little extra insurance.

Another advantage is that vegetables and fruits, particularly when eaten raw, require time to be chewed, which helps satisfy oral crav-ings. Also, fruits and vegetables just don't taste good with cigarettes and are unlikely to trigger the urge to smoke.

Water, Water Everywhere

Both smokers and quitters should drink large quantities of water, preferably eight or more glasses a day. Two-thirds of the human body is made up of water. The body loses a lot of water every day through basic functions. If this water is not replaced, dehydration results.

Just as they need more vitamins, smokers need to drink more water than the average person. Unfortunately, most smokers drink a lot less water than even the six glasses per day recommended for people who haven't been smokers.[3] Water aids the kidneys by routinely flushing out toxins, but smokers have more toxins in their bodies, which forces the kidneys to work harder. Without adequate amounts of water, the kidneys can't do their job properly. Poisons build up and can cause serious problems, such as bladder cancer. Drinking at least eight glasses of water each day can significantly reduce a smoker's risk of developing this type of cancer. It also improves the skin and enhances overall health.

In smokers who are trying to quit, drinking a lot of water is a great way to speed up nicotine withdrawal. It takes only three to five days for nicotine to completely leave the system (it takes longer to form new habits—more about that in **Step 12: Driving on the Wrong Side of the Road**), but drinking water can speed up the process and diminish withdrawal symptoms. Drinking water can also be used to satisfy oral cravings so your smoker doesn't stuff her face with food when the urge for a cigarette hits. Again, developing the habit ahead of time will make quitting easier once that happy day arrives.

The Milky Way

Dairy products are another food group that doesn't go well with cigarettes. Many smokers associate smoking with a morning cup of coffee or evening cocktail, but cigarettes with a glass of milk? Never!

Dairy products are high in calcium. Smoking is a risk factor for osteoporosis, a loss of bone density that causes disability, even death, in many older adults. Adding calcium to the diet can prevent osteoporosis. But the poisons in cigarette smoke prevent the body from absorbing calcium. Your smoker may already suffer from a calcium deficit because of smoking. Now is the time to build up the bones with calcium-rich dairy products and help reduce cravings at the same time.

A word of caution: Whole milk and ice cream are high in fat, which should be reduced during the transition from smoking to nonsmoking. It's best to drink skim or reduced-fat milk and to choose frozen yogurt or fruit-flavored sorbet in place of ice cream. If your smoker is lactose intolerant, soy milk works just fine, but urge him to stick with the low-fat or fat-free versions.

Our Daily Bread

Adding whole-grain cereal, bread, and pasta to the diet reduces the likelihood of constipation that many ex-smokers complain about immediately after quitting. Whole grains do not trigger the desire to smoke, and like other plant-based foods, they help reduce cravings.

Avoiding Triggers

Some foods and beverages increase the desire to smoke. These include sugar, strong spices, and foods containing high amounts of fat, particularly red meat, along with alcohol and beverages containing caffeine (coffee, tea, hot chocolate, and some soft drinks). Many smokers associate cigarettes with coffee or cocktails or with lighting up after a big meal, which, in the United States, often consists of red meat with lots of starches, few vegetables, and a rich dessert. This type of diet affects the metabolism and blood-sugar levels in ways that can make cigarette cravings worse.

Alcohol is particularly risky for quitters because of what I call the "what-the-hell" syndrome. Especially in the early stages of quitting, alcoholic beverages can cause smokers to relax their guard or eliminate their resolve to quit, especially if there are other smokers nearby.

If your smoker has a problem with alcohol (this is not uncommon among hard-core smokers), this problem should probably be resolved before attempting to quit smoking. Studies of recovering alcoholics who quit smoking indicate that addiction to alcohol is easier to master than addiction to nicotine. Alcoholic beverages nearly always trigger the desire to smoke, but smoking doesn't necessarily trigger a desire to drink.

There are many good resources available for the treatment of alcoholism in the form of recovery programs and support groups such as Alcoholics Anonymous. The coping skills smokers learn in these programs can only help them conquer an addiction to tobacco.

It's Only Temporary!

When you talk to your smoker about limiting or avoiding certain foods and beverages, be sure to let her know that this doesn't mean *forever!* With the exception of smokers who have a problem with alcohol and should therefore eliminate it entirely, the dietary changes listed above are intended as a temporary measure. I'm always careful to emphasize the word *temporary* whenever I facilitate stop-smoking classes. Smokers tend to live in the present, and quitters, who are already giving up something that affects every aspect of their lives, are usually horrified at the thought of giving up everything all at once. Be sure to let your smoker know that giving up red meat, coffee, and chocolate isn't *permanent.* (I personally consider chocolate one of the four basic food groups.) Once your smoker has developed new habits, she can go back to eating hamburgers, spicy enchiladas, and chocolate bars. A funny thing sometimes happens, though. Quitters, in the process of rediscovering their taste buds, often discover that they *like* fruits and vegetables and aren't always eager to resume old dietary patterns. The payoff is twofold: They stop inhaling all the dangerous toxins in cigarette smoke and start consuming more vitamins and minerals, which can help prevent cancer and other serious illnesses. Their bodies will applaud them, and so should you!

If the smoker you care about is someone you live with, you might introduce the idea of dietary changes by making changes in your own diet. Tell your smoker you've been reading some of the nutritional guidelines that suggest consuming five servings a day of fruits and vegetables and ask him to join you in your quest for better health. If you're in charge of the cooking, make sure vegetables and fruit are part of all meal preparations. If the smoker is a friend or co-worker, buy him a cookbook that emphasizes healthful, innovative ways of preparing fruits and vegetables. Visit a farmer's market together and have fun selecting the freshest produce you can find. Be sure to mention that eating more vegetables and fruit enhances weight control as well as makes giving up cigarettes easier.

Some cessation programs claim that certain foods or vitamins in various combinations can help smokers quit. There is little scientific basis for these claims. However, there is no harm in encouraging your smoker to eat a well-balanced diet and follow some of the basic rules of good nutrition, which include eating five or six small meals daily rather than three large ones. Eating more frequently also helps avoid the drop in blood sugar that causes many smokers to crave cigarettes.

⤷ Chapter Thirteen ⤶

STEP 10: WHAT TO EXPECT WHEN YOUR SMOKER QUITS
Action Stage

As your smoker's quit date approaches, you may be torn between elation and dread. Everyone has heard horror stories about the agonies quitters endure, not to mention the hell they put everyone else through. (I once read a story about a newspaper reporter who quit for the Great American Smokeout and ended the day by putting his fist straight through a shower stall!) Everything from hallucinations to hair loss has been attributed to smoking withdrawal. But with a little forethought and gentle management, your smoker's experience need not be as horrendous as either of you may fear.

It's important to note that not all smokers experience withdrawal. People using nicotine replacement or antidepressant therapy report fewer withdrawal symptoms than those who don't. Some even claim they have no withdrawal symptoms whatsoever. But if the smoker you care about is of the hard-core variety, I wouldn't depend on that, even if your smoker uses Zyban, the patch, or both. Remember that this is withdrawal from a drug that's both highly toxic and severely addicting. You can probably count on anything from a rough couple of weeks to a tough couple of months.

The good news is that even the worst cravings usually last only a minute or two, and the worst of these will subside within two weeks or less. It takes anywhere from months to years to learn new habits and coping mechanisms (more about that in **Step 12: Driving on the Wrong Side of the Road**), but that's not what you're worried about now. Your immediate concern is what to expect in those first few crucial days after your smoker quits.

Don't be surprised if your ex-smoker reports some unusual symptoms. I've heard ex-smokers attribute to smoking withdrawal everything from blurred vision to mouth sores. (One smoker's mouth sores turned out to be caused by the consumption of five bags of cinnamon candies in a single day!) Anything that sounds alarming should be reported to a doctor. But for the most part, what your ex-smoker goes through in those first few days or weeks is not only normal but actually part of the healing process. Below are some of the more common symptoms, along with suggestions about how to deal with them.

A strong craving or urge to smoke: This is the most obvious symptom. The good news is that most of these cravings are self-limiting. They'll disappear in a minute or two if the ex-smoker just waits them out. If she can't do that (or thinks she can't, which is the same thing), remind her that she can go for a walk, work out at the gym, practice deep breathing, drink water or fruit juice, say a prayer, or take a nap. In short, do anything *except* give in to the urge. That is the one and only thing she absolutely must not do.

Feeling light-headed or dizzy: All this means is that your ex-smoker's brain is getting more oxygen than it's used to receiving. Usually, it takes only a couple of days to make the adjustment. Tell your ex-smoker to exercise caution behind the wheel of a car or while operating machinery until symptoms subside. If your ex-smoker feels like he's going to pass out (or actually *does* pass out), he may need to consult a doctor.

Difficulty concentrating or paying attention: More oxygen is reaching the brain. Advise your smoker to be kind to herself for a couple of days. Her ability to concentrate will return before long.

Tingling sensation or numbness: This means your ex-smoker's circulation is improving. These sensations may be uncomfortable but rarely are painful and will disappear with time. I experienced a pins-and-needles feeling in my hands when I first quit. I also noticed that the palms of my hands, which were usually bright red (a sign of poor circulation), had turned a nice, healthy pink. All this happened in the first few days—one more sign of just how quickly my body was willing to forgive the abuse I had subjected it to for all those years.

Irritability, anxiety, restlessness, frustration, or anger: These are typical symptoms of drug withdrawal. For relief, suggest exercise, deep breathing, getting plenty of rest, and above all, asking others to be patient. You may have to tiptoe around your ex-smoker for a few days, but be assured that the symptoms will pass.

Trouble sleeping: Suggest deep breathing, soothing music, warm milk, or herbal tea at bedtime. Avoiding caffeine is a must, as is refraining from heavy physical exertion late in the day. Check with a doctor if insomnia persists, as this could be a symptom of an underlying depression. (See **Step 13: Consider the Link between Smoking and Depression.**)

Lethargy or listlessness: This is another sign of recovery. It's similar to the kind of fatigue you feel when you're recovering from an illness. It means the body is healing itself. Tell your ex-smoker to get a little extra rest and try to be patient. Before he knows it, he'll have more energy than ever before.

Trouble with bowels: Your ex-smoker's body may have become dependent upon the shock of nicotine to jump-start its natural functions. These functions will return to normal with time. It helps to add fiber to the diet (whole grain breads and cereals, fresh fruit, and vegetables). Regular exercise and drinking lots of water can also aid regularity. A mild laxative may be helpful on a temporary basis.

Hunger or craving for sweets: Your ex-smoker has been accustomed to putting something in her mouth hundreds of times every day. These cravings may have less to do with actual hunger than with the need for oral gratification. Sucking or chewing on a straw, cinnamon stick, or toothpick may satisfy the urge. I even knew one ex-smoker who quit with the help of a baby's pacifier! If the cravings are a result of genuine hunger, tell your ex-smoker to eat something, for heaven's sake! Five or six small meals a day are better than three large ones to keep blood-sugar levels under control. If your smoker craves sweets, suggest fruit, which is high in natural sugar. Strawberries, apples, melons, and peaches can satisfy an overactive sweet tooth. Fruit juice is another source of natural sugar, but be careful not to overdo this as it is also high in calories. Drinking plain water is always a good choice. One of my favorite beverages during my last quit cycle was cold water spiked with a little lemon juice and artificial sweetener. Chewing sugar-free gum or sucking on hard candy can also provide relief.

Cough: Many newly minted ex-smokers are dismayed to find that they cough a lot in the first few days or weeks after quitting. This is especially discouraging if they've never before experienced a smoker's cough. Believe it or not, this is another healing sign. What it means is that the cilia (tiny hairs that clean the lungs) were paralyzed by cigarette smoke. Now they're coming back to life. Rejoice! Your ex-smoker's body is ridding itself of tar and other toxins trapped in his lungs. Try honey and lemon juice or mild cough drops if the cough becomes problematic. It will likely disappear in another week or two. If it persists beyond two or three weeks, consult a doctor.

Headaches: Some ex-smokers report headaches in the first day or two after quitting. This is both a withdrawal and recovery symptom, resulting from the absence of nicotine, the presence of enhanced circulation, and the removal of toxins from the body. Encourage your ex-smoker to drink at least eight glasses of water each day and take aspirin or other over-the-counter pain relievers as needed. If the headache lasts beyond two or three days, check with a doctor.

Tightness in the mouth or throat: This was a symptom I experienced every single time I quit. I learned it was caused by muscle tension. In my case, tension was focused on the mouth, which, being accustomed to lots of attention, apparently felt neglected. The tightness can also be caused by too much candy or chewing gum, which can cause jaw muscles to become overworked. Brushing the teeth seems to help, as does rinsing with a nice, minty mouthwash. Deep breathing can also be beneficial, as can herbal tea or other warm beverages. Keep in mind, however, that coffee or other caffeinated beverages should be avoided in the early stages of quitting.

Dry mouth: The obvious solution is to drink plenty of water. Keeping a bottle of water always on hand is advisable for anyone going through nicotine withdrawal. Drinking water also helps flush nicotine out of the body and usually speeds recovery. (Buy spring water, if you prefer. It's less expensive when purchased by the case.) Sugarless gum or hard candies also help, but water really is the best remedy.

Following are a few stress management techniques that you can suggest to your ex-smoker when tension, irritability, or craziness from withdrawal get out of hand.

Deep breathing: As stated earlier, smokers are used to inhaling and exhaling deeply hundreds of times each day. These are usually deep, satisfying breaths, despite the poisons smokers manage to inhale with each one. But people who are feeling stressed tend to take short, shallow breaths. Not only is your ex-smoker dealing with the stress of withdrawal, she's also probably missing the satisfaction of all those deep breaths she used to take.

Deep breathing is a great stress buster for people who have just quit smoking, not only because it recreates an activity they're used to performing hundreds of times each day, but also because it's relaxing and satisfying in and of itself. I use this technique whenever I have to do a media interview or deal with some other stressful event in my life. It's simple and unobtrusive enough to do anywhere at any time. Try it yourself. Anyone can benefit from this exercise.

Begin by standing or sitting as straight as possible. The head and neck should also be straight, but the neck muscles should be loose and flexible. Keeping the mouth closed and lips relaxed, breathe in slowly through the nose. Force the air all the way down to the base of the diaphragm, pushing the stomach outward as more breath is inhaled. Continue to inhale as much air as possible to a count of seven. Close your eyes and hold for a count of five. Then exhale through the mouth to a count of seven, feeling the stomach deflate as all the air is released.

Urge your ex-smoker to do this exercise before doing anything else whenever he feels a craving for a cigarette. It can be repeated as often as necessary until cravings pass.

Relaxation exercise: Your ex-smoker can read the following instructions into a tape recorder to play it back whenever she needs relief from stress or tension. You might also offer to read it aloud while she sits in a comfortable chair or lies on a sofa or bed. Before starting this exercise, draw the blinds or curtains and unplug the phone to avoid interruptions. If you like, play some soothing instrumental music. Read slowly and distinctly, allowing plenty of pauses between each instruction.

"*Close your eyes and tense your feet, from toes to ankles. Contract the feet and hold. Relax. Now tense the thighs. Contract the feet, calves, thighs, and hold. Relax. Now tense your abdomen. Contract the feet, calves, thighs, abdomen, and hold. Now tense the shoulders and arms. Contract the feet, calves, thighs, abdomen, shoulders, arms, and hold. Relax. Now tense your neck. Contract the feet, calves, thighs, abdomen, shoulders, arms, neck, and hold. Relax. Finally, tense the muscles of your face and scalp. Tense all the muscles throughout your entire body as tightly as possible. Hold for a count of ten: one . . . two . . . three . . . four . . . five . . . six . . . seven . . . eight . . . nine . . . ten. Very slowly, let all the muscles of your body relax. Relax your scalp. Relax your face. Relax your neck and shoulders. Relax your abdomen, legs, and feet. Feel everything go limp. Continue to breathe deeply. In through the nose. Out through the mouth. Slowly breathe in. Hold. Now slowly breathe out. Right now you are at peace. At this moment you have no problems or worries. You feel peaceful and completely relaxed.*

"*While continuing to breathe slowly and deeply, picture yourself in a beautiful, serene setting. Maybe you see yourself in a deep, green forest. Perhaps you're beside a sparkling waterfall. Maybe you're on a beach at sunset or a mountain path beside a clear, blue lake or a gurgling stream. Make the scene whatever you want it to be. Picture* the details. See it clearly. Smell the sweet, clean air; see and smell the flowers; hear birds singing; feel a warm, gentle breeze caress your skin. See yourself on the grass or the warm sand, or on a soft bed of pine needles. Look up at clouds passing overhead in a bright, blue sky. Feel the beauty of this place. Know that it is real. Feel it. Believe it.

"Now take another deep breath, allowing the air to pass through your nose and throat into your lungs. Feel your lungs fill with clean, pure air. Slowly exhale. Feel the air pass from your lungs to your throat into your mouth and out into the atmosphere. You are totally relaxed. You are completely at peace. Life is good. You feel great. You are healthy, happy, and relaxed. As you experience this good feeling, know that you are a worthwhile person. Know that you are strong and confident. You deserve good things. You deserve to be a nonsmoker. Believe in this feeling. Know that it is real. Feel it in your bones, skin, and all your muscles as the sun beats down on you in your special, magic place. Slowly breathe in through your nose and hold, then slowly breathe out through your mouth. Breathe in again through the nose. Hold it. Now breathe out through the mouth. Now open your eyes, feeling completely relaxed and tension free."

Gifts for encouragement: Your ex-smoker will certainly appreciate a gift from you during these first few difficult days and weeks. Because most ex-smokers worry about gaining weight after quitting, non-food items are best. You might consider buying him a gift certificate for a relaxing massage. (Depending upon the nature of your relationship, you might offer to provide the massage yourself.) Another appropriate gift is a basket containing aromatherapy oils and lotions, herbal tea, scented candles, and tapes or CDs of soothing music.

The most important gift you can offer, however, is your encouragement and support. There's no need to overdo it, but let your ex-smoker know how proud you are of her courage and strength during this tough transition. Keep reminding her that all the tension, irritability, stress, and strain of this experience are only temporary. Someday soon, it will all be just a memory. In the meantime, remind her to be kind to herself. Be extra gentle with her until the worst of her withdrawal symptoms have passed.

☙ Chapter Fourteen ❧

STEP 11: FIND BIRDS OF A DIFFERENT FEATHER FOR YOUR SMOKER TO FLOCK WITH

Action Stage

You've probably heard the expression "Misery loves company." Few people care to think of themselves as spreading misery or negatively influencing others. But negative feelings can get the better of the best of us, and there are times when we don't even understand why.

Human beings are social animals. We all need to feel accepted by others. One of the best ways to ensure that we are accepted is to gravitate to those with values, tastes, and habits like our own. Chances are that a large percentage of your ex-smoker's social circle are smokers. In this day and age, when few nonsmokers are willing to tolerate the dangers and discomforts of secondhand smoke, that's especially likely to be true.

Being around smokers puts your ex-smoker at greater risk for relapse. It also gives him less incentive to quit. Sometimes other smokers feel threatened by someone who quits. Some ex-smokers even report that their quitting makes friends and family who still smoke react with anger or hostility. These people may feel threatened or envious. When someone else quits, it forces those who still smoke to confront their denial or their own desires to quit. They may fear the creation of another nonsmoking fanatic who will try to persuade them to quit before they're ready. At the least, friends and family who continue to smoke are not likely to be supportive of the person you care about once he makes the transition from smoker to ex-smoker. At worst, they may try to undermine him or persuade him to start smoking again.

Support and encouragement are vitally important to any recovering addict. Fortunately, your ex-smoker has a supportive element in her life—you. You can help steer her away from potential saboteurs by introducing her to fun, interesting, understanding nonsmokers. Being around people who don't smoke not only provides additional incentive for smokers to quit, it also provides them with an additional source of support once they do.

This is not to say that you have to eliminate all smoking influences from your ex-smoker's life. That may not be either practical or possible, especially if these are people he lives or works with or who are relatives or close friends. This is simply about expanding his social circle to include more nonsmokers. Fortunately, this encompasses about 77 percent of the adult population in the United States. Rather than giving up anything, your ex-smoker will actually be broadening his social horizons to include this enormous variety of potential new friends and acquaintances.

Hopefully, your own social circle already includes a large number of nonsmokers. If so, introduce your ex-smoker to those you think she might like. Plan to do something she normally enjoys doing with her smoking friends. Naturally, all of you will insist upon enforcing the clean-air rule during the time you are together. If you select places where smoking is not allowed, this will be easier.

For smokers who remain part of your ex-smoker's life, try discussing the situation with everyone involved. If possible, try to involve them in your effort. Those whom you sense to be a particular threat may be taken aside so you can say, "I know you care about John as much as I do. He just quit smoking, and I'm trying to encourage him. I'm really concerned about his health."

You're not lying, not even a little bit! Your ex-smoker's health will likely suffer if she starts smoking again, and you have every right to be concerned. If individuals really care about your ex-smoker, they're not likely to engage in acts of sabotage, especially when the subject is broached in this manner. People who smoke tend to be more sensitive about the danger to others than they are to themselves, so putting it in these terms may inspire their protective instincts. Despite misgivings, they may appreciate the opportunity to be part of the effort.

Suggest to your ex-smoker that he ask other smokers not to smoke around him once he quits. Point out that his good example may inspire others to follow suit. Share with him some of the methods you've learned in this book to help his smoking friends break their own deadly addiction to tobacco. Ask him to practice positive responses in advance if a smoker tries to undermine his efforts. Encourage him not to let anyone interfere with his resolve to be the best he can be. Above all, make sure that you yourself do not undermine his efforts to quit.

"What?" I can almost hear you shouting. "Why on earth would I sabotage her when I want so much for her to quit?" Remember what I said earlier about change? It is frightening for most people, even when it's a change for the better. I can just about guarantee that you will see changes in your ex-smoker after she quits, and not just in her health. You will also discover changes in her personality. Some of these may not be to your liking.

Addicts can be creative when it comes to forcing problems into the recesses of their subconscious minds. Smokers are no exception. It's easy to ignore situations that cause stress and strain if, when stressful situations arise, you can light a cigarette and make all your problems go up in smoke. Keep in mind that times of stress and strain are times when smokers traditionally crave cigarettes most. Most people prefer the path of least resistance. It's a lot easier to smoke than to deal with the causes of these stresses and strains.

I practiced this form of avoidance for years. Instead of dealing with the problems in my life, I sat and smoked. Instead of confronting friends and relatives who said or did things to hurt me, I would go off somewhere and smoke cigarettes until my hurt feelings became bearable. Another ex-smoker told me about the depression she suffered after a death in her family. Instead of dealing with her grief, she sat in her kitchen and smoked. Her decision to quit came once she realized that all her free time was spent in that kitchen, creating a smoke screen between herself and her grief. Once she quit smoking, she finally felt the pain she'd been avoiding, thereby initiating the process of healing.

Once I quit smoking, I forced myself to make some tough choices. I also began confronting people who hurt me. Some of these were people who had been nagging me about my smoking for years. Though they were glad to see me quit, they had certainly not considered confrontational behavior to be among the benefits! All of this was hard, both on me and on those with whom I began to work through old conflicts. Nevertheless, by confronting these issues, I was finally able to make progress in resolving them.

Quitting smoking is a major life change. More often than not, it leads to a chain reaction. Your ex-smoker may begin to assert himself, possibly for the first time in his life. A lot of bottled-up resentment may come pouring out. Some of that resentment might be directed toward you. It may help to remember that this is part of a natural and highly desirable healing process. Alcoholics Anonymous talks about the need for those in recovery to deal with issues they've been avoiding with the help of alcohol. Recovery from tobacco addiction is no different. Unless your ex-smoker deals with some of the issues that have kept him addicted, he is in grave danger of returning to cigarettes for comfort. He needs to develop new coping mechanisms and work through problems he may never have confronted before. A support group such as those offered by Nicotine Anonymous can help him learn better ways of dealing with stress and anxiety. But while he's learning, you may be in for a bumpy ride.

Try not to be defensive if some of the pent-up anger and resentment she expresses is directed at you. Try also not to be overly analytical about these feelings. It may be that some of her anger is justified. It may be that you're just handy. The most likely answer is that she's trying to gain control of her life.

Most smokers have no idea what it's like to be adult non-smokers. For most of his life, the ex-smoker you care about relinquished control to cigarettes. Now he's trying to find himself under the layers of addiction. It may be that the person he finds is different from the person you thought he was. Try to deal with him as he is instead of judging him by who he used to be. This may almost be a bigger challenge for you than it is for him. Try to remember that people are constantly in the process of changing. Quitting smoking may have sped up a process that, sooner or later, probably would have occurred anyway. But now he may actually live long enough to enjoy it!

Your ex-smoker deserves to be free of the shackles of nicotine dependency. Help her believe that nothing and no one—not even you—should stand in her way.

⟩ Chapter Fifteen ⟨

STEP 12: DRIVING ON THE WRONG
SIDE OF THE ROAD
Maintenance Stage

The Appian Way of the road to a smoke-free lifestyle is strewn with ex-smokers who relapsed. Most people assume that if a smoker manages to quit for a couple of weeks, he or she has the problem licked. That assumption couldn't be more wrong. In fact, the relapse rate remains extremely high for months after quitting. Between 80 and 90 percent of smokers who quit relapse sometime in the first forty-five days. For some people, the relapse risk continues to be a problem for as much as a year or more. There are even a small percentage of ex-smokers who manage to stay away from cigarettes for a decade or longer until a major crisis hits—the death of a close family member, a serious illness, even retirement—and they fall back on old, destructive patterns.

Yes, Just One Will Hurt!

When your ex-smoker first started to smoke, it probably took weeks, months, even years to develop the habits connected with smoking. Those first few puffs likely made him dizzy, light-headed, and sick to his stomach. This was due to the effects of nicotine and other chemicals such as arsenic, formaldehyde, ammonia, carbon monoxide, hydrogen cyanide, and dozens of other deadly poisons. For someone unaccustomed to these toxins, dizziness and nausea is a common side effect. But the human body is amazingly adaptive, sometimes to its own detriment. After a while the body adapts to the poisons at the same time it builds up a tolerance for nicotine. Because nicotine is so addictive, the body soon requires more of the drug to maintain comfortable tolerance levels until it reaches a set point. As we learned in previous chapters, this is the amount of nicotine the addict must have each day to avoid withdrawal symptoms. Nicotine can be washed out of the body in just three to five days, but the set point remains the same, regardless of the amount of time your ex-smoker has been tobacco-free. Just one puff of a cigarette will trigger the set point and place your ex-smoker right back at the starting line. Sooner or later, that one cigarette will lead your ex-smoker back to a pack a day. It will be as if he never quit at all.

The Ex-Smoker's Bermuda Triangle

One common time for relapse is what I call "the ex-smoker's Bermuda Triangle." Ex-smokers generally fall into this black hole in the first few months after quitting. It's one reason why the success rates of many stop-smoking programs are often skewered. When you hear about a smoking cessation program that claims a 50- to 75-percent success rate, ask how long the program runs. Most stop-smoking classes run about four to six weeks, with the first classes beginning a week or two before the smoker's actual quit date. This means that at the end of a month, ex-smokers are cast adrift in a terrifying world with which few are prepared to cope. Think about programs like Alcoholics Anonymous or other drug rehabilitation programs that addicts participate in for years. These successful programs achieve their success because they understand the nature of addiction. They understand that an addict is *always* an addict. Support must be ongoing for it to be truly effective.

For smokers, support often ends after just a few weeks. Unfortunately, this is right about the time an ex-smoker's initial motivation and enthusiasm begin to ebb. It's the time when friends and family, in the mistaken belief that the ex-smoker has the problem under control, relax their guard. It's the time when prescriptions for stop-smoking medication, if any are used, run out. It's also the time when an ex-smoker is most likely to encounter a crisis. Smokers tend to schedule quitting efforts during times in their lives that are relatively low in stress. However, life being what it is, stress always returns, and the ex-smoker usually finds herself facing some sort of crisis within a few months of her quit date. It may or may not be a serious crisis. It may even be a crisis she has dealt with successfully in the past. The problem is that she has probably never dealt with most adult life situations without cigarettes. This behavior pattern must change if she is to remain an ex-smoker.

Learning to Drive on the Wrong Side of the Road

Remember that most smokers start smoking in their teens. Unless your ex-smoker has managed to quit for long periods of time in the past, he probably has no idea what it's like to be a nonsmoking adult. He has no clue how to deal with normal life situations without the so-called stress relief of cigarettes. Of course, as we've already learned, cigarettes don't relieve stress—they increase it. But while your ex-smoker's intellect may accept this idea, the addict that lives within him may tell him otherwise. His automatic reaction during stressful times has always been to reach for a cigarette. Not having a cigarette to reach for can create panicky feelings that catch many ex-smokers unprepared.

If you've never smoked, it may be hard to understand how a normally competent, rational adult can be so dependent on a piece of crushed vegetation wrapped in chemically treated paper. Let's try to find an analogy to which you can relate. Since most smokers start smoking in their teens, think about something both you and your ex-smoker learned to do as teenagers that now feels automatic. Let's take learning to drive a car as an example.

Chances are, learning to drive didn't come automatically. It takes time to learn to coordinate steering, turning, using the brake or the clutch, parking, backing up, accelerating, decelerating, keeping an eye out for other traffic, watching your speed, even adjusting the radio. With enough time and practice, these reactions became automatic. Most people don't think about each step as they're driving. They may be focusing on traffic, directions, even the scenery, but the actual mechanics of driving are second nature to an experienced driver.

Now, let's say that after learning to drive in the United States, you move to England. In England, the steering wheel, brake, clutch, and everything else you're used to finding on the left side of a car are now on the right. Instead of driving on the right side of the road, you're supposed to drive on the left. At first, this will feel terribly awkward, but with enough practice you can unlearn the old way of driving and grow comfortable with new driving habits. Then let's say you're driving along some English lane one day when a truck suddenly pulls out in front of you. What are you going to do? Well, we know that stressful situations often cause us to return to old habit patterns. In an emergency, American drivers in England have been known to swing the steering wheel to the right. This, of course, can create serious accidents with potentially tragic results.

The secret of learning to drive on the wrong side of the road is to prepare for crisis situations in advance and to practice appropriate responses until they feel natural. To use the analogy with smoking, this means being aware of potential relapse risks and practicing resistance skills. Relapse risks include:

- Giving in to the temptation to try "just one"
- Alcohol use
- Being with friends who smoke
- Being surrounded by smokers at work or home
- Feelings of deprivation and boredom
- Celebration or reward
- Serious or prolonged stress

Feeding the Monster

Giving in to the temptation to try "just one" can easily lead to relapse. This is a dangerous test and usually means the ex-smoker has either failed to learn new adaptive responses or is kidding herself about how addicting even one cigarette can be. Ex-smokers need to remember that addiction may be controlled but can never be eradicated. Like a recovering alcoholic, the ex-smoker must stay away from cigarettes completely. Once an addict, always an addict; with addiction there are no halfway measures.

One method some ex-smokers find helpful is a visualization technique I use with participants in my stop-smoking classes. Tell your ex-smoker to imagine that the addict who lives within him is a Monster. Like all living creatures, the Monster requires nourishment. Every time your ex-smoker feeds the Monster by smoking a cigarette, it gains strength and power. But if he starves the Monster by denying it sustenance (cigarettes), eventually it will grow weak and lose its power.

It's important to keep in mind that the Monster never dies. It will always be part of your ex-smoker. But as long as she doesn't feed the Monster, it won't have the power to control her.

Encourage your ex-smoker to try this exercise if you think it will help him. Some people find it too "New Age," but others find it enormously helpful. If your ex-smoker does decide to try it, you can help him during times of stress or hardship with a gentle reminder not to feed the Monster. You may even want to make a poster, like a sign at a zoo, that reads: "Don't feed the Monster!" and place it somewhere your ex-smoker will be sure to see it. Sometimes this is all it takes to distract a craving that's getting out of hand and to get your ex-smoker back on track again.

Alcohol

We've already determined that alcohol should be avoided or eliminated in the early days of quitting. But even after those first few agonizing weeks have passed, alcohol remains a danger to ex-smokers. Drinking at parties where other smokers are present can create an overwhelming temptation. Alcohol tends to lower resistance and creates an apathetic attitude in some people. This can mean the end of a long cycle of resolve and determination by giving in to the temptation to give the Monster just a tiny, little snack. Just one, as you know, means back to square one.

Others' Smoking

Being around friends and family members who smoke frequently triggers relapse. The apparent freedom and enjoyment observed in others who smoke may trigger memories that can be hard to resist. Watching a co-worker smoke or seeing a family member smoke can create a mind-set of, "Well, if others are doing it, it must be all right." The ex-smoker sees only the momentary pleasure rather than the long list of negatives that probably led her to quit. Inhaling secondhand smoke may also provide the brain with enough nicotine to induce a craving for cigarettes.

I now refuse to share space with someone who is smoking. When a smoker lights up in my presence, I either ask him or her to put the cigarette out, or I get up and leave. I try to ask politely, explaining that I have a problem with cigarette smoke. This happens to be true. I *do* have a problem. It's called addiction, and this recognition creates an automatic aversion that enables me to avoid the substance to which I am addicted. I know that I am only one cigarette away from being a smoker again. For my self-preservation, I am determined to avoid that one cigarette.

Deprivation and Boredom

Feeling deprived or bored can trigger relapse in people who live alone or for whom cigarettes were their only companion. A quit-smoking group or some other type of group therapy may be useful for these people. Another positive alternative is to volunteer for the American Cancer Society or another nonprofit organization that will reinforce your ex-smoker's determination to stay away from cigarettes.

Celebration or Self-Reward

People often relapse when good things happen. Being on vacation, being at a party, or sharing with old friends, especially if those friends smoke, often creates another kind of "What the hell!" attitude. This is similar to the feelings mentioned above, of not wanting to be deprived. Most ex-smokers regret giving in to temptation once the situation has passed, especially when they realize they have to start all over again. It's helpful to find rewards other than cigarettes that an ex-smoker can set aside in advance.

Stress and Other Negative Events

Stress is one of the most common reasons ex-smokers cite for falling off the tobacco wagon. Situations that create anger, tension, or fear often create a desire to smoke in someone who has quit. In the past, your ex-smoker may have dealt with unpleasant emotions by creating a smoke screen. Rather than deal with whatever he felt, he probably reached for a cigarette. A smoker who is feeling stressed will usually light a cigarette before doing anything else. Without cigarettes, the ex-smoker has two problems: Stress and the fact that he can't use a cigarette to cope with it.

It may not even be a big problem that causes the ex-smoker to crave cigarettes. Anything from an argument with a spouse to unexpected expenses can provoke the desire to return to old coping methods. Anger is particularly dangerous, as the ex-smoker may reach for a cigarette out of a desire to punish the person she is angry with. However, the regret most ex-smokers experience as a result of relapsing is usually pronounced and often much worse than the original emotion.

"Flu Shot" against Relapse

Get out a piece of paper. On that page, list the relapse situations mentioned above. Leave about an inch to an inch and a half of space between each one. Then hand the list to your ex-smoker and ask him to come up with an appropriate nonsmoking response to each one of these situations. He may be able to think of other situations that caused him to reach for a cigarette during past quit attempts. If so, ask him to list these and to come up with appropriate nonsmoking responses.

Resist the urge to come up with these responses for her. All you should present her with is a list of the most common situations that cause smokers to relapse. Because the response has to be something that feels right to her, logically, it should come from her. Remember, she still has to do the heavy lifting. You're only there to cheer her on.

Obviously it is impossible to imagine everything that could possibly go wrong for the rest of your ex-smoker's life. But by developing this list, he will have a wide variety of nonsmoking responses from which to choose in the event of an unanticipated crisis. I tell participants in my stop-smoking classes that making this list is like getting a flu shot against relapse. Not only can it lessen your chances of getting the flu, but also, even if you catch it, you're likely to get a lighter case, and you'll probably recover much faster.

What to Do If Your Ex-Smoker Falls Off the Wagon

She should get right back on! Everyone makes mistakes, but a single mistake does not have to mean failure. Rather than let one cigarette lead to a pack, encourage your ex-smoker to start over. Remind her of the reasons she wanted to quit smoking. She may go through some withdrawal, but with the nicotine of just one or even a couple of cigarettes in her system, it won't be as bad as when she first quit.

Avoid, at all costs, making him feel like a failure. He probably feels guilty enough as it is. Tell him nobody's perfect. Let him know you still believe in him. Remind him that he is now an *ex*-smoker. Remind him of all the advantages of not smoking. And help him get back on track again.

☙ Chapter Sixteen ❧

STEP 13: CONSIDER THE LINK BETWEEN SMOKING AND DEPRESSION
Maintenance Stage

There are smokers who try again and again to quit. Each time they try, they become so moody and difficult to live with that family and friends may actually encourage them to start smoking again. These smokers may be genetically predisposed to depression.

My own experience validates this theory. Every time I tried to quit smoking, I experienced such feelings of despair and emptiness that I occasionally entertained thoughts of suicide. I always associated these feelings with cigarettes, or to the deprivation I felt because I'd given them up, though doctors kept trying to discover a connection to some other stressful event in my life.

Scientific studies about the link between mental illness and nicotine addiction were first published in the 1990s, though it's only been recently that the medical community as a whole has paid serious attention. Smoking cigarettes alters levels of different chemicals in the brain, affecting mood, feelings, and emotions. It may also explain why people with depression, schizophrenia, and other psychiatric disorders are more likely to smoke.[1] When it comes to depression, it's still a question of what came first: Does smoking cause depression or do people start smoking to relieve its symptoms? Some scientists believe that the poisons in cigarette smoke change the brain's chemistry and may actually cause mental illness. Others believe depression comes first and that smoking is a form of self-medication.

Not only are people with a tendency toward depression more likely to be smokers,[2] but also a history of major depressive disorders have been associated with lower success rates among smokers who enter smoking cessation trials.[3] In the mid-1990s, the FDA approved the first antidepressant recommended specifically for smoking cessation. This drug, called bupropion (also known by the trade names Zyban and Wellbutrin), works by raising levels of chemicals like dopamine, a feel-good substance naturally produced by the brain. Nicotine also stimulates dopamine. Smokers with a history of depression who consistently fail to quit may actually be craving dopamine stimulation.[4] Tobacco just happens to be one source of the drug their bodies are missing.

Fortunately, there are medications that provide the same feel-good chemicals without the disease-causing agents of tobacco. The use of Zyban, in conjunction with a tobacco counseling program, appears to more than double a smoker's chances of quitting successfully. In one study, 49 percent of Zyban users quit smoking for a month versus just 36 percent of those who used a nicotine patch. (Only about 3 percent succeed going cold turkey with no quit-smoking aids.) Using both the patch and Zyban, 58 percent of smokers were able to quit for a month.[5]

The long-term quitting rates are less dramatic but equally encouraging. In a study at the University of Wisconsin, nearly one-third of smokers who used Zyban were able to stay off cigarettes for at least one year, as opposed to just 16 percent of patch users. Subjects who used both Zyban and the patch had slightly improved long-term success rates, but the use of Zyban appears to be the crucial element for successful quitters.[6]

More than once, depression caused me to start smoking again after quitting successfully for months at a time. Fortunately, by my twelfth quit attempt, I had enough experience to recognize these symptoms for what they were. After I was put on a low dose of antidepressants, I experienced unbelievable relief. I also experienced a few side effects, including fatigue, listlessness, dry mouth, and stuffy sinuses. But when I compared the side effects of the medication to the side effects of smoking (which include death!), I decided the medication was preferable. I stuck with it, despite my grogginess and dry mouth. To my pleasure and surprise, a few months after I started taking the drug every one of the medicine's side effects disappeared.

If your ex-smoker seems unusually sad, lethargic, or down after quitting, she should consider the possibility of depression. In all likelihood, this condition was present before she quit, but the self-medication of smoking may have masked her symptoms. These symptoms include:

- Persistent sad or empty mood
- Loss of interest or pleasure in ordinary activities, including sex
- Decreased energy, fatigue, feelings of being slowed down
- Sleep disturbances (insomnia, early-morning waking, or oversleeping)
- Eating disturbances (appetite and weight loss, or weight gain)
- Difficulty concentrating, remembering, making decisions
- Feelings of guilt, worthlessness, helplessness
- Feelings of "Who cares?" or "Why bother?"
- Thoughts of death or suicide, or even suicide attempts
- Irritability
- Excessive crying
- Decreased productivity at work or in school
- Lack of cooperation
- Safety problems, accidents
- Chronic aches and pains that don't respond to treatment
- Alcohol, drug abuse, or other addictive behaviors

Everyone feels depressed sometimes. Life tends to weigh down even the hardiest souls. For most people, depression is a fleeting emotion that's linked to a specific situation. But for some people, depression is not linked to a particular life crisis. It is a physical ailment, like diabetes or heart disease that, if left untreated, can be just as serious. Of all depressed people, 15 percent commit suicide as a result of their depression. Two-thirds of all suicides are directly related to depression.[7]

If the ex-smoker you care about suffers from depression, he is certainly not alone. One in twenty Americans currently suffers from a depression severe enough to require treatment. One person in five is estimated to suffer from depression at some time in life. About 2 percent of all children and 5 percent of adolescents also suffer from depression.

One reason why it's so much harder for women to quit smoking is that they appear to suffer more often from depression. More than twice as many women as men are treated for depression, but it's not known whether this is because women are more likely to be depressed or because men are less likely to ask for help. Whatever the case, women seem to fail more often when they attempt to quit smoking and fail earlier in the quit cycle. Another factor may be concern over weight gain. Women tend to be more concerned about physical appearance than men are, and even the few pounds of weight gain normally associated with giving up cigarettes can cause panic in some women. Of course, gaining weight only adds to their depression.

I can't remember a time when I didn't suffer from depression. Before I received treatment and for a long time afterward, my depression was a source of shame, both for me and for my family. Everyone, myself included, felt that if I could just pull myself up by my socks and get on with life, I would snap out of it. What we all failed to understand was that depression is an organic illness. It is the result of a chemical imbalance in the brain that I could no more snap out of than I could snap out of cancer. All I knew was that smoking made me feel better. So I kept smoking, even though I felt horrendous guilt because of my failure to quit. But I knew that for me, it was either smoking or suicide, though smoking was just a slower form of suicide.

Despite my own past ignorance, I am always astonished at the large number of people who consider depression a lack of character, discipline, personal strength, or common sense. Some of these are members of the health professions. Depression carries a stigma that burdens few other illnesses. Many people still believe that getting help for depression implies a lack of fortitude or gumption. They think that if only they could get their act together, everything would fall into place. But seeking help for an illness has nothing to do with character or strength. It actually takes a great deal of strength to consult trained professionals for advice and direction when something goes wrong. Depression is a treatable illness, and there is no virtue to suffering in silence. Besides, people who suffer from depression rarely suffer in silence. Depression is an equal-opportunity illness. Everyone gets to suffer along with the depressed person.

If depression affects your ex-smoker, chances are better than average she's also abused other drugs such as alcohol. Like cigarettes, alcohol is a socially acceptable drug. It's also a common, self-prescribed medication for depression. Like cigarettes, alcohol is a depressant. After the initial rush, or euphoria, it intensifies the depression. Drugs of all kinds—legal, illegal, over-the-counter, even the nice drugs doctors prescribe—are often used in unsuitable ways by depressed people. These drugs do not solve the problem. They only make it worse.

Your ex-smoker may react defensively when you suggest that depression is the reason he still craves cigarettes or the reason he smoked in the first place. This is a common and unfortunate reaction. It used to be that people who suffered from depression were considered weak or crazy. Some people still believe that. I look at it this way: If a person had diabetes, he wouldn't be ashamed of needing to be on insulin, would he? So why would anyone be ashamed of needing medicine for depression?

If you think the ex-smoker you care about is suffering from depression, don't take my word for it; seek professional help. Your family doctor may be a good place to start. Hopefully, your doctor will refer you to someone who is trained in the treatment of mental illness. If it turns out that the ex-smoker you care about *does* suffer from depression, it is likely she will be given a prescription for anti-depressants. Please encourage her to stay on the medication, even if it means she has to experiment with different dosages or medications until she finds the right treatment.

I originally considered placing this step first rather than thirteenth because smokers who suffer from depression may need to begin antidepressant therapy before they will be receptive to the idea of giving up cigarettes. This is especially true if your ex-smoker has already tried to quit at least once before. However, I placed it near the end because the feelings smoking can mask often become apparent only when the smoker gives up his crutch. Then and only then will he recognize that something is needed to shore up his defenses.

Some antidepressants take six to eight weeks before the effects are noticeable. Until then, your ex-smoker may not be capable of recognizing the connection between the harrowing feelings depression can cause and the lingering desire to smoke. That's why it's usually better to start antidepressant therapy at the beginning of a stop-smoking attempt. Most doctors recommend starting Zyban at least one week before the actual quit date. But getting this kind of treatment is advisable if symptoms of depression become noticeable at any time during the quit cycle. It's also another way to dramatically increase your ex-smoker's chances of staying quit, not to mention giving her a whole new lease on life.

Trust me—antidepressants are a much more effective way to treat depression than cigarettes and a lot less expensive, too.

◈ Chapter Seventeen ◈

STEP 14: CELEBRATE WHERE YOU ARE

Relapse Stage

A woman once called my office at the American Cancer Society for information. She had emphysema and chronic respiratory disease. Her doctor had informed her that if she didn't quit smoking, she wouldn't live another year.

"The thing is," she qualified, "I *like* smoking. I really don't want to quit. Can't you give me something to make me *want* to quit?"

"Madam," I answered dryly, "if we had something like that, we'd put it in the water supply!"

This woman had tried numerous quit-smoking methods but was disinclined to try any of them again and argued with every new suggestion I made. By the time she hung up, all I really wanted to know was whether she had a good lawyer who could help her make a will. She had made up her mind before she picked up the phone. Smoking meant more to her than prolonging her life. Who was I to question her choice?

Sometimes, no matter how hard you try, no matter how faithfully you execute all the steps laid out in this book, the smoker you care about will either refuse to try or fail so often he simply gives up. You should prepare yourself for that possibility. Remember what I said earlier: You can't force change in another person. The only person you can change is yourself. So if the smoker you care about is unable to quit or refuses to try, all you can do is decide how *you* will cope with that. The choices, as I see them, are fairly straightforward.

1. You can give up on the idea of helping him quit and live with him as he is.
2. You can give up on the individual and sever the relationship.
3. You can keep trying.

If a person who smoked was someone I really cared about, my choice would probably be to keep trying. But I can't make that choice for you. Only you can do that. Whatever you decide has to be right for you and your circumstances.

If you choose the third option, one thing you might find helpful is to celebrate where you are. It's a matter of looking for the positive in whatever circumstances you and your smoker happen to find yourselves in.

Say, for example, that as a result of your following the steps laid out in this book, your smoker cuts down on the number of cigarettes she smokes each day. That's cause for celebration! Congratulate her for minimizing the toxins in her body and tell her you know this will make it easier to quit when and if she decides to do so.

Let's say your smoker agrees to smoke outside so you won't be bothered by secondhand smoke. Thank him for his consideration and recognize that by making it more difficult for him to smoke, he is bound to smoke fewer cigarettes. Eventually, he may become so fed up with the inconvenience that he simply decides to quit.

Keep in mind that people change at different rates of speed. Your smoker may not respond as quickly as you would like but that doesn't mean she'll never be ready to quit. People are constantly changing. Just about the time you're ready to throw in the towel, your smoker may surprise you by announcing that she's ready to quit.

There are some situations in which I would not recommend even attempting to persuade a smoker to quit, such as that with the woman I described at the beginning of this chapter, for example.

Quite obviously her mind was made up. It wouldn't have been worth the time or energy involved. Another example was presented to me by a family friend whose father was ninety-two years old at the time and a smoker (one of those exasperating exceptions smokers are so fond of pointing to when others talk about the health risks of smoking). My friend wanted to know how to persuade her dad to quit smoking. I answered that as long as he wasn't smoking in her presence or in the presence of other nonsmokers, I really didn't think it was worth the effort. The man, after all, was ninety-two! Anyone over the age of seventy-five has probably already suffered the worst that cigarettes can do to them, and they're not likely to live long enough to enjoy most of the health benefits of quitting. So unless there is some compelling reason for them to quit, the best course is to let them be.

In working with smokers, I often find it helpful to think of the Serenity Prayer used by Alcoholics Anonymous: *"God grant me the serenity to accept the things I cannot change, the courage to change the things I can, and the wisdom to know the difference."* That last part is probably the great challenge—knowing the difference. But if it isn't possible to change your smoker, it's always possible to change yourself. As long as you continue to follow at least the first five steps, there's still hope that your smoker will react to the changes in you. Those steps, in case you've forgotten them, include:

Step 1: Don't nag!
Step 2: Redirect your anger.
Step 3: Clear the air.
Step 4: Empower your smoker.
Step 5: Overcome the fear of failure.

Even if you manage to follow only the first three steps, you will accomplish several things. First, you will reduce your smoker's resentment by not nagging him to death. Second, you will be able to deal more effectively with your anger. Finally, you will protect yourself from secondhand smoke. Even if your smoker never quits, all of this can only work to the good.

A popular philosophy states: "Be grateful for what you have, and more will follow." Once we learn to celebrate where we are, at whatever time and place we happen to be, new vistas have a way of magically appearing before us. Wherever you happen to be, remember the following fable. It may hearten you when you begin to feel that all is lost.

One day both the Sun and the Wind spied a man wearing a heavy overcoat. The Wind made a bet with the Sun that he could make the man remove his overcoat. The Sun decided to take the bet and calmly sat back to watch.

The Wind blew as hard as he could in his effort to blow the coat off the man. But the harder the Wind blew, the more tightly the man clutched the overcoat around him until finally, out of breath, the Wind gave up.

"Mind if I try?" asked the Sun.

"Be my guest," said the Wind.

The Sun smiled and beamed down with all her might. After just a minute, the man wiped his brow and gazed up at the sky. Then he took off his coat, threw it over his shoulder, and continued on his way.

Be like the Sun. Beam down with light and warmth. Before you know it, that special someone you care about will be ready to throw off the dangerous addiction known as smoking and travel on toward a happier, healthier future.

❧ Part III ❧

ᓯ Introduction ᓆ

After reading through the previous sections, you may have found yourself thinking, "The person I care about doesn't really fit into any of these categories, so maybe none of these steps applies." Maybe the person you care about isn't a smoker at all but a chewer. Perhaps the smoker you care about is pregnant and you're concerned that this approach for helping someone quit smoking will take too long and result in too much damage to the unborn baby. Maybe the smoker you care about is a teenager or preteen child. Perhaps you're a teenager or preteen yourself, and you're worried about a parent who smokes. Maybe you're even wondering why a substance as dangerous as tobacco is still permitted to be openly marketed and sold and how the industry that sells it ever came to occupy such a powerful position in our society.

All tobacco addicts have elements in common. If, for example, you're concerned about someone who chews tobacco, the steps for helping smokers quit would also apply, though chewers have their own distinctive problems. If the smoker you care about is a pregnant woman or an underage user, these individuals still have to deal with the same psychological and physiological problems of other tobacco addicts, but either age or condition creates a sense of urgency. In the next few chapters, I try to cover as many of these unique circumstances as possible. However, as stated in the introduction to the previous section, the guidelines presented here are suggestions rather than edicts. They are tools to help you find your own answers and help you forge a better understanding with the tobacco user you care about.

ꙅ Chapter Eighteen ꙩ

EMERGENCY MEASURES

A relaxed, step-by-step approach to help a smoker you care about quit may not be appropriate with every smoker. There are some situations in which age or circumstances create a state of emergency. Two such situations are highlighted below.

When the Smoker You Care about Is Pregnant

Pregnancy is one situation in which the consequences of smoking are both immediate and potentially catastrophic. Compelling evidence demonstrates that smoking during pregnancy can adversely affect the developing fetus and the health of the baby after birth. Studies have shown that women who smoke have:

- Greater risk of pregnancy complications
- More stillbirths
- A 20-percent higher rate of miscarriage
- Babies who die soon after birth because of low birthweight[1]

The carbon monoxide in cigarette smoke causes a decrease in the blood's oxygen supply. In a pregnant woman, this oxygen-poor blood circulates through the fetus and robs the fetal tissue of the nutrients needed for growth and development. Studies have also shown that nicotine builds up in the placenta and is then passed on to the fetus, which is why nicotine replacement therapy is not a good option for most pregnant women.[2]

The harmful effects of smoking during pregnancy do not end when the baby is born. Long-term studies have shown that when mothers were heavy smokers during pregnancy, children tended to be shorter than their peers, were slower readers, and had more difficulty adjusting to social situations than children of nonsmoking mothers. Differences in behavior and school placement were also demonstrated.[3]

The more cigarettes a pregnant woman smokes, the greater the risk to the fetus and to the child after it is born. Mothers who smoke ten or more cigarettes per day increase the chances of their children developing cancer by as much as 50 percent, particularly cancers such as leukemia or lymphoma.[4]

Talk about innocent victims. How could any mother live with the guilt if her child died of cancer and she knew herself to be the cause? To my eternal shame, I smoked when I was pregnant. My son, thank God, has good social skills, average intelligence, and above-average health. Nevertheless, knowing what I now know, if he is ever diagnosed with any form of cancer, I will never forgive myself.

The effects of smoking during pregnancy have tragic consequences for babies. Newborns whose mothers smoke during pregnancy have the same nicotine levels in their blood as adult smokers and almost certainly spend their first few days of life going through withdrawal. Some scientists have even concluded that babies whose mothers smoked during pregnancy should probably be considered ex-smokers.[5]

An obstetrical nurse once told me that it's easy to spot the babies in the hospital nursery whose mothers smoked. The withdrawal that nicotine-addicted babies suffer is similar to the symptoms displayed by crack babies. They cry continuously, refuse to eat or sleep, and fuss or flail about when somebody tries to hold or comfort them. It's heartbreaking to watch and even more heartbreaking to realize what they must be suffering.

Continued exposure to cigarette smoke after birth can cause additional developmental difficulties. It can also cause an increase in respiratory illnesses and higher mortality rates due to sudden infant death syndrome (SIDS). Children with asthma are especially prone to health problems because of exposure to secondhand smoke. Several thousand children die from complications of asthma every year. A high percentage of these complications have been directly linked to cigarette smoke.[6]

Anything and everything that can be done to help a pregnant woman quit smoking should be done without delay. The longer a woman smokes during pregnancy, the greater the risk to the unborn baby. Suggested strategies include:

- Enlist the aid of your pregnant smoker's obstetrician. This type of assistance should be part of all prenatal care. All too often it is not. Other than repeating warnings about the risks of smoking during pregnancy, few physicians take an active role in helping their patients quit. Unfortunately, only about 20 percent of pregnant women who smoke are able to quit on their own.[7] This percentage could easily be doubled if more physicians would offer such simple assistance as educating pregnant patients about relaxation techniques or behavioral strategies. Even something as simple as providing a list of reputable stop-smoking programs can make a world of difference.

  Busy doctors sometimes feel they don't have time to counsel patients about stop-smoking techniques. But just three minutes of counseling by physicians can double the quit rate of patients who smoke. Ten minutes or more of physician counseling can triple the quit rate.[8]

  Talk to your pregnant smoker's obstetrician. Tell him or her about your concerns. Make sure the physician is not simply advising your pregnant smoker that she *should* quit. She should be told by someone whose authority she respects that she *must* quit. When it comes to pregnancy, there is no room for debate about smoker's rights

or individual choices. It's not just her life she's gambling
with now. The life of her baby is also at stake. The baby, we
can all agree, is far too young to be smoking.

- If the obstetrician won't or can't help, find a doctor who
  can and will. This might be a family physician or internist
  who is well trained and skilled in smoking cessation techniques. The doctor who treats her pregnancy doesn't have
  to be the same doctor who treats her for nicotine addiction.

  It is highly advisable that your pregnant smoker receive
  this support from a doctor or another health care provider.
  This person can deliver vital information to your pregnant
  smoker and give her help in ways you cannot possibly provide. Why? Because if it comes from you, it'll seem like
  nagging. If it comes from a doctor, it carries the weight
  of authority.

- Pregnant smokers may want to try acupuncture, hypnosis,
  aromatherapy, massage, or herbal teas that provide relaxing or soothing effects. Encourage your smoker to try
  anything that won't adversely affect the developing fetus.
  Natural remedies are best, but keep in mind that even
  herbal teas sometimes contain elements that may be
  harmful to an unborn baby. Again, always seek a doctor's advice before attempting any treatment.

- As stated earlier, smokers often show more concern when
  their behavior is a health risk to someone else. The threat
  of damage to an innocent baby may do the job all by itself.
  Nonaccusingly, ask your smoker if she can live with the
  guilt if her child develops leukemia or lymphoma. Ask her
  if she thinks she'll blame herself if her baby suffers brain
  damage or has learning disabilities.

- If your pregnant smoker remains unconvinced that she
  is harming either her child or herself, it might help to
  remind her that child abuse charges have been brought
  against women who have caused irreparable damage to
  their unborn babies by using cocaine or alcohol during
  pregnancy. Some studies have implied that the damage

to an unborn baby from the toxins in cigarette smoke are
equal to or greater than the risks of cocaine use during
pregnancy.[9]

When the Smoker You Care about Is Underage

If you discover that a preteen or teenaged child is smoking, treat
this discovery as if you had just learned that he is in the grip of an
extremely dangerous drug, because he is!

The fact that U.S. kids smoke more than one billion packs of
cigarettes each year is alarming for several reasons.[10] First, the
younger people are when they begin to smoke, the harder it will be
for them to quit and the likelier it is that they will die of a tobacco-
related disease.[11] Second, seductive tobacco marketing still aimed
at young people (despite its having been outlawed through the tobacco settlement) can override adult objections or their own common sense. Third, and most alarming of all, recent studies indicate
that teen smoking may result in genetic damage that may not be re-
versible, even if they quit soon afterward. The younger people are
when they start, the more damage is done. Tobacco-related cancer
may show up as much as twenty to thirty years later. So, even a brief
period of experimentation with smoking can come back to haunt
these kids in the form of lung cancer in later life.[12]

Much of society still perceives smoking as a relatively harmless,
albeit irritating, habit, at least in comparison to the use of more serious drugs such as marijuana or cocaine. Many school districts
still have designated student smoking areas that allow kids to develop the habit of smoking and reinforce the addictive powers of
nicotine. Sales of tobacco to minors continue despite laws that make
it illegal to sell tobacco products to anyone under the age of eighteen. All of these things combined make it ridiculously easy for a
young person to become enslaved to tobacco.

The tobacco industry has long depended upon the naiveté and
susceptibility of what they euphemistically refer to as "young adult"
smokers. Unfortunately, their idea of a young adult differs quite a

bit from yours and mine. Recently released industry documents reveal that some tobacco executives regarded potential customers as young as twelve years old to be "young adults."[13] Though industry spokespeople have been quick to declare that references to twelve-year-olds were merely errors in documents turned over to the courts, the evidence proclaims otherwise. The most convincing evidence is the effect that cigarette marketing has had on the very age group they still insist they never targeted.

There is still a lot we don't know about the problem of youth tobacco use, but there are a few things we do know. One of these is that tobacco is a gateway drug, meaning there is a strong correlation between tobacco and other drug use. According to the 1994 Surgeon General's report, kids who smoke are three times more likely than nonsmokers to use alcohol, eight times more likely to use marijuana, and twenty-two times more likely to use cocaine.[14] Other studies have demonstrated that kids who start experimenting with cigarettes at age eleven or younger are twice as likely to engage in other types of risky behavior as kids who don't smoke.[15]

Threatening kids with the potential health risks of smoking has little, if any, effect. Traditional prevention programs that emphasize tarry lungs and cancerous cells leave most young people unimpressed. If anything, these tactics have resulted in increased rather than decreased youth smoking rates. If smoking is perceived as risky or dangerous, what better incentive could there be for a young person enthralled with the romance of daring or risky behavior? Clearly, the denial that keeps so many adult smokers hooked is even more pronounced in young people.

Another thing we know is that poor self-esteem or a negative self-image plays a vital role in whether kids start smoking. Other risk factors include:

- Lower levels of academic achievement
- Friends who use tobacco
- A parent or sibling who uses tobacco
- Lack of skills that help them resist influences to use tobacco

- Lack of involvement in school or community activities (athletics, band, church, etc.)
- Depression or other mental illness

In talking to your children about tobacco use, emphasize the cosmetic effects rather than health hazards. Talk to them about bad breath, stained teeth, foul-smelling hair and clothes, and most teens preferring to date someone who doesn't smoke. Remind your children that smoking will make them perform poorly in competitive sports, cause problems when playing a musical instrument, and affect cheerleading and speech. If your child shows any symptoms of depression, have her evaluated by a qualified psychologist or psychiatrist. Above all, treat the problem of tobacco use as seriously as you would treat any other drug use.

If you discover that your child is using tobacco, you may want to consider one or more of the following actions:

- *Cut off financial resources.* Kids can't purchase cigarettes without money. If this means stopping allowances or forcing your child to quit a part-time job until you are convinced he has stopped smoking, this might be what you have to do.
- *Find out if your child's friends smoke.* Chances are pretty good they do. If this is the case, let these parents know that their kids are smoking. What other parents decide to do about this is not your problem. You will have done your duty by passing along the information. Allow your child to entertain her friends only under your supervision or the supervision of someone you trust until you are certain she is no longer smoking.
- *Discover the source of supply.* Where is your child buying his cigarettes? Wherever it is, remember that it is against the law throughout the United States to sell tobacco products to anyone under the age of eighteen. Find out what enforcement measures are in place in your city or state. Invoke these measures if you can. If enforcement is sketchy

or halfhearted (this, unfortunately, is the case in many places), make certain the managers or owners of the stores your child patronizes are aware that you know they've been breaking the law by selling tobacco to minors. The threat alone often compels retailers to take better precautions. If your child is buying his cigarettes from someone at school, report it to the school authorities. The sale or resale of individual cigarettes ("loosies") is also illegal in most states, and disciplinary action should be taken against anyone who is doing this.

- *Does your child's school have a student smoking area?* If so, ask your school board to eliminate it. It may be necessary to make a lot of noise about this. Schools are often surprisingly reluctant to deal with the problem of tobacco use. They see this as a family matter rather than a school problem. In fact, it's everybody's problem.
- *Enlist the aid of your family physician or other health care provider to help your child quit smoking.* Though nicotine replacement therapy and other stop-smoking methods recommended for adults are often not appropriate for youth, some doctors will weigh the risks of smoking against the potential benefits of stopping and prescribe these drugs for smokers under eighteen. If you think your child suffers from depression and is smoking to mask the symptoms, suggest this to your doctor and see if antidepressant medication might not be part of the answer.
- *Have your child's urine tested.* Because nicotine shows up in the urine, urinalysis is one way to be absolutely certain whether your child is still smoking. However, I would recommend this only in hard-core cases, as it's usually best to try to foster an atmosphere of trust. Still, if you've tried everything else without success, ask your doctor about testing your child's urine. Your child will at least know you're serious.
- *If people in your family smoke, ask them to quit as a positive example to your child.* Above all, do not allow anyone to

smoke in your home or in the presence of your child. Kids need to see that you are willing to hold others to the same standards you demand from them.

In addition to discipline, children who smoke need positive reinforcement to stay away from cigarettes. Positive reinforcement techniques include:

- *Separate the behavior from the individual.* Although you should certainly express disappointment and make it clear that you will not tolerate your child's continued use of tobacco, let her know that you value her. Make sure your child knows you love and appreciate her for who she is, even though you disapprove of something she's done.
- *Help your child improve his social skills.* Teach refusal techniques like those taught in drug prevention classes. For example, *Diversion:* "No, thanks, I'm on my way to a movie. Want to come along?" *Assertion:* "Smoking is gross. I don't want to poison myself with tar and nicotine." *Humor:* "A cigarette? No, thanks, I can live without it!"
- *Encourage and assist your child in meeting her goals.* Does she want to join the softball team? Spend some time playing catch with her and help her develop her athletic skills. Does she dream of being a dancer or a model? Spring for ballet or tap lessons or investigate modeling classes.
- *Express interest in your child's activities.* Congratulate successes, no matter how small. Above all, congratulate him for trying! Let him know you believe in him and you'll always be there to cheer him on.
- *Keep criticism to a minimum.* One of the most challenging things we do as parents is to keep loving our children even when they're not lovable. It's also the most important thing we'll ever do in our lives. Try to find something positive in everything your child does and remember the old axiom: If you can't think of anything nice to say, don't say anything at all.

- *Take your child's ideas and emotions seriously.* Acknowledge that their problems are just as real as your own. Adolescent traumas may seem silly to you, but keep in mind that adolescents haven't had time yet to develop the emotional and intellectual resources that you have. Also keep in mind that you were young once, too, and probably resented it when adults belittled *your* worries and concerns.

What about my previous insistence on not forcing change in others? A child is different from a spouse, parent, sibling, or friend. As parents, we are responsible for our children's physical, emotional, and spiritual welfare. The time will inevitably come when you must allow your child to make her own choices and suffer whatever consequences those choices bring. But as long as she is living under your roof, you don't have to allow her to do something that has an excellent chance of killing her.

Kids need our love and support, but it's important to adopt an overall attitude of zero tolerance when it comes to smoking, one of the toughest addictions to overcome. It may also lead to other addictions and almost certainly will result in health problems unless you lick the problem early. Remember, one out of three kids who starts smoking today will die of a tobacco-related disease. You are well within your rights as a parent to do everything in your power to ensure that your child doesn't become one of them.

ꙮ Chapter Nineteen ꙮ

FOR KIDS WHOSE PARENTS SMOKE

Every year, on the third Thursday in November, the American Cancer Society reminds people about the dangers of smoking and encourages them to quit for at least one day. The celebration is called the Great American Smokeout, an annual event sponsored by the American Cancer Society. I received a letter from a twelve-year-old girl who saw a tobacco presentation I had arranged at her middle school.

Dear Ms. Melin:

I saw your program at my school the day of the Great American Smokeout. Ever since then I've been worried about my dad. My dad smokes, and after what I learned about tobacco, I'm really scared something terrible will happen to him. I love my dad, and I don't want him to die from lung cancer or a heart attack.

Christmas is coming, and the only gift I want is for my dad to quit smoking. I'm putting together a "Quit-Smoking" kit that I plan to give him as a Christmas present. (In a way, it's really a present for me!) I'm going to put things like gum, candy, toothpicks, rubber bands (so he'll have something to do with his hands), and herbal tea in it. Can you help by sending me some stop-smoking brochures, pamphlets, or maybe posters to put in the kit? Maybe you can think of something else I could put in there. I would appreciate any help you can give me.

Very truly yours,
Jennifer Smith*
* Name changed to protect privacy

The day after I received this letter, I wrote the following response:

Dear Jennifer:

I think your "Quit-Smoking" kit is a wonderful idea! It's hard to imagine a father who would not be deeply moved by such a gift. I'm enclosing the brochures you asked for. If I could suggest anything else for your kit, I would strongly recommend the letter you wrote to me. (I'm enclosing a copy so you can include it.) There's a lot of good information in these brochures that can help your dad quit smoking once he's ready. I'm also enclosing a list of stop-smoking classes for your dad to look over. But along with the list and brochures, I'd like to offer you a little advice.

As I'm sure you know, quitting smoking is very hard to do. In fact, some people think it's harder to quit smoking than it is to quit drinking or using drugs like cocaine and heroin. I know how hard it is because I used to be a smoker. I tried and failed to quit smoking eleven times before I finally succeeded on my twelfth attempt. I remember so well how guilty I felt whenever my son begged me to quit smoking. I also remember how he would cry and how angry he was when I failed. I understood his anger. I even understood his tears. At the same time, it made me feel guilty. Feeling guilty always made me feel anxious and stressed, and that just made me want to smoke more.

Jennifer, your dad probably feels guilty, too. He probably wants to quit even more than you want it for him. He may have already tried to quit one or more times in the past. Hopefully, he learned something from that experience, but starting to smoke again probably made him feel like a failure. That feeling of failure may make him afraid to try again.

There are several things you can do to help your dad. Your "Quit-Smoking" Kit is a great place to start. Wonderful as this is, however, don't be surprised if your dad tells you he doesn't feel ready to quit just yet. If he does, don't get mad or nag him about it. Instead, see if you can't work out a bargain with him. The first thing to do is ask him not to smoke around you. Secondhand smoke is dangerous for nonsmokers, especially for someone your age. Tell your dad that you'll respect his right to smoke, but he must respect your right to breathe clean air. Ask respectfully, but don't hesitate to make this request of him. Your dad will probably smoke fewer cigarettes as a result, and you'll be protecting yourself at the same time.

The second part of your bargain is that you will support him when he's ready to quit. Hopefully, he'll listen to your concerns and will read some of the information you've included in your kit. It's okay to share your fears about smoking. But be sure you're telling him what *you* fear and what *you* feel, not what you think *he* should do. You probably don't like it very much when your folks tell *you* when to be home, when to do *your* homework, when *you* have to go to bed. Well, your father is the same. Nobody likes to be told what to do. It's better if the idea comes from him. As much as you want this for him, he has to want it for himself for it to work!

The most important thing you can do is to keep telling your dad how much you love him. Let him know that you'll be there to help him when he's ready to quit. Tell him that you realize how hard it is to quit smoking but that you think he has the strength and courage to do it. It's important to let your dad know that you believe in him because that gives him the best reason in the world to quit. How could any father not do everything in his power to live up to that kind of faith?

Once your dad is ready to quit, encourage him to set a quit date, maybe a week or two from the time he decides to quit. The reason for the delay is that a week or two before he quits, he may want to visit your family doctor. The doctor can talk to him about patches, gum, or pills that can make it a lot easier for him to quit smoking. Make sure your father knows that it's not a sign of weakness to ask for help with quitting. Everyone needs a little help now and then. Quitting smoking is hard enough without having to prove how tough you are!

When your dad *does* quit, be sure to live up to your end of the bargain. Be on your best behavior for the first two or three months, or at least until he gets the stop-smoking jitters out of his system. Remember that what he's going through is very, very hard. Tell him over and over again how proud you are. Tell him you *know* he can beat this problem. Above all, be sure to remind him that you believe in him.

If he should start smoking again (of course you hope this won't happen, but sometimes it does), try not to get too upset. Most smokers try and fail many times before they finally quit. Encourage your dad to learn from his mistakes and urge him to try again as soon as possible. Congratulate him for trying. Above all, encourage him to *keep* trying.

Jennifer, your father is very lucky to have a daughter like you. Keep me posted and please let me know if there's anything else I can do to help.

I wish you and your family a very Merry Christmas and a healthy, happy New Year. Good luck, Jennifer, and God bless.

Sincerely,

Barbara

Barbara White Melin

৩ Chapter Twenty ৎ

WHEN THE PERSON YOU
CARE ABOUT CHEWS TOBACCO

Little information is available for chewers who want to quit, even less for those who care about someone who chews. The main reason for this scarcity is that many people consider chewing, or smokeless, tobacco safer than smoking. What image comes to mind when you think of smokeless tobacco? Doesn't it just *sound* safer? After all, where there's no smoke, there's no fire, right? That's why tobacco control experts insist upon using the term *spit tobacco* rather than *smokeless* or even *chewing tobacco*. They think this more accurately reflects what the product is all about.

Because spit tobacco doesn't produce secondhand smoke, it's considered less of a public nuisance—that is, unless you're sitting next to someone in a theater or airplane who is spitting slimy brown juice into an empty cup or soda can. However, even this is generally categorized alongside scratching your armpit or picking your nose in public. Uncouth, perhaps, but if somebody wants to run around with brown spittle dripping out of his mouth, who are we to judge?

My home state of Colorado has the unhappy distinction of having the third highest spit-tobacco use rate in the nation. (Our neighbors in Wyoming are tied with West Virginia for first place.) As with the increase in cigarette smoking by young people, the fact that spit-tobacco use proliferates in Marlboro Country is no coincidence. Rodeos and stock shows receive millions of sponsorship dollars from the companies that produce Skoal, Copenhagen, and other spit-tobacco brands. Professional baseball's record is also dismal. For many years, baseball stars with huge wads of spit tobacco parked against one or both cheeks were paid enormous sums of money to help tobacco producers advertise these products. Fortunately, with the help of organizations like the National Spit Tobacco Education Program (NSTEP), baseball has begun to demythologize spit-tobacco use. Former Yankees great Joe Garagiola has made this issue a personal crusade. As NSTEP's national spokesperson, he travels around the country persuading baseball players to set a better example for the young men and women who idolize them.

Think back to the story about Sean Marsee from chapter nine. In many ways, Sean was a typical spit-tobacco user. He started chewing when he was just twelve years old. This, unfortunately, is not at all unusual. The average age for beginning spit-tobacco use is nine. Like a lot of spit-tobacco users, Sean was from a western state, Oklahoma. Like many chewers, he was a baseball fan who played the game himself. His baseball coach wasn't alarmed by his use of spit tobacco: After all, it wasn't as if he was doing something really harmful, like smoking. Sean paid a high price for this ignorance. He died at the age of nineteen, just seven years after he started using spit tobacco. So much for the notion that only old people die of tobacco-related illness.

When I worked for the Colorado Dental Association, I heard of other cases like Sean's and many more instances of chewers in their teens and twenties losing most or all of their teeth because of the harsh abrasives in spit tobacco. I heard of others diagnosed with leukoplakia, a precancerous condition characterized by hard, white patches on the tongue and roof of the mouth. Often, these conditions require extensive surgery. To prevent tragedies like Sean's, surgeons sometimes have to mutilate patients by removing gums, teeth, lymph nodes, even jaws to save their lives.

Remember what I said in the introduction to Part I: Spit tobacco is still tobacco and every bit as deadly. It doesn't cause lung cancer, but cancers of the mouth and throat are common with spit tobacco, as is every sort of dental disease imaginable. Because of the high nicotine levels in spit tobacco, it's also a risk factor for heart disease and stroke. There's actually a higher concentration of nicotine in spit tobacco than in cigarettes. Somebody who goes through a can of spit tobacco every day gets the same amount of nicotine as a six-pack-a-day smoker.

It's fairly common for smokers to wean themselves from cigarettes with spit tobacco. This reminds me of the old saying about insanity being defined as continuing to make the same mistake, yet expecting different results. Tobacco addiction cannot be cured with tobacco. It's just trading one danger for another.

If you know someone who uses spit tobacco, he (or she—an increasing number of girls and women chew these days) has a serious problem. In addition to nicotine withdrawal, spit-tobacco users often have to deal with oral gratification needs that can be difficult to overcome. For the most part, the same guidelines apply to chewers as to smokers. Spit-tobacco users can use Zyban or nicotine replacement therapy to deal with their addiction. Chewers may also require some kind of oral substitute until they learn new habits and attitudes.

One product I first heard about when I worked for the dental association was called Mint Snuff, a mixture of crushed mint leaves and a noncavity-causing sweetener called sorbitol. It comes in several flavors (including mint) and is available at most drugstores, usually in the tobacco products section. You can also order it by calling 1-800-EAT-MINT or on the Internet at: www.mintsnuff.com.

Some chewers do just as well with sugar-free gum, hard candy, or other oral substitutes. It's really a matter of personal preference. The important thing to keep in mind is that, with spit tobacco, you're dealing with two distinct problems: An addiction to spit tobacco's nicotine that may be as severe, if not more severe, than to that in cigarettes, and the need to keep something in the mouth to replace the quid of spit tobacco.

ᕲ Chapter Twenty-One ᕰ

THE POLITICS OF TOBACCO

"I want you to consider anew the disgraces of the
tobacco wars and ask you: Where is the outrage?"
From a speech by Dr. C. Everett Koop, National Press Club,
Washington, D.C., September 8, 1998

"People who start to smoke are well aware of the risks and willingly
assume them."

"Cigarettes are not addictive."

"Cigarette makers have done nothing to keep smokers hooked."

"Tobacco companies have not halted or attempted to hide research about the safety of their products."

"There's no scientific proof smoking causes illness."

"Tobacco companies have never marketed to children."

"The tobacco industry opposes youth smoking."

This is a sample of the testimony offered by tobacco company
representatives during class-action lawsuits filed by smokers and the
families of dead smokers. On the face of it, these arguments are
ridiculous enough to insult the average eight-year-old. Nevertheless,
throughout the history of these lawsuits, juries have seldom ruled
against the tobacco industry. Even when verdicts have gone against
Big Tobacco, judges have overturned most of them on appeal.

"What about personal responsibility?" I hear people say. "How is
it that smokers can indulge in behavior they know is dangerous,
then turn around and sue the tobacco industry when a risk they

willingly assume catches up with them?" I'm all for personal responsibility. The premise of this book, as well as every piece of advice I've ever offered on this subject, has to do with smokers taking responsibility for their choices. If they choose not to do the heavy lifting—the hard work involved with quitting—they must bear the consequences of death, disease, and social ostracism.

But smokers are not the only ones who must bear these consequences. Millions of family members and friends watch in helpless silence as someone they care about succumbs to a dangerous and often untreatable addiction. Millions of taxpayers bear the burden of increased public health costs. Millions of workers pay higher health insurance premiums so that insurance companies can pay the extra medical expenses smokers incur. Above this landscape, remote and strangely removed, is an industry that manufactures a product known to kill one out of every three consumers, an industry that has covered up the truth about its product's dangers, an industry that has corrupted our political system to protect the industry's right to go on selling the product. What's missing in most discussions about personal responsibility is an examination of a carefully orchestrated campaign of lies, manipulation, and greed that symbolizes the dark side of our national character.

The conduct of the tobacco industry over the past fifty years is an example of capitalism run amok. It represents the avarice eroding our society and the cynicism with which many Americans now regard our government. Other industries whose products have endangered human life or safety have long since been regulated or forced to comply with public safety standards. But Big Tobacco has escaped responsibility by buying and lying its way out of practices that would land the average citizen in jail.

The tobacco industry has enjoyed profits beyond the fantasies of ordinary mortals while engaging in practices that for decades were kept hidden from public view. Then the state of Minnesota brought a lawsuit against the tobacco industry and uncovered a wealth of documents that confirmed the wildest nightmares of health advocates. These documents prove that tobacco industry researchers and executives knew about the health risks of smoking and were engaged in an elaborate conspiracy to mislead the public about those risks. They prove that the industry was fully aware of the addictive nature of nicotine and worked hard to exploit that potential. And they demonstrate beyond a reasonable doubt that children were targets of tobacco industry advertising and promotions.

For years, tobacco industry spokespeople have sputtered angry denials in response to charges that they marketed to kids. These denials continue despite the evidence contained in millions of documents now filed away in a Minnesota warehouse. Like wayward children with jam-smeared faces who insist they've been nowhere near the jam, the tobacco industry has followed a bizarre system of lying, loudly and with considerable chest-thumping, to everyone from Congress to consumers. However, since the documents came to light, their system has developed some embarrassing kinks.

For a long time, public health advocates based assumptions on purely circumstantial evidence, though these were certainly damning enough. We believed, for example, that the industry's claims of advertising only to convince adults to switch brands was a fallacy. Repeated studies had shown that adults rarely switched brands, but the three most heavily advertised brands, Camel, Marlboro, and Newport, also happen to be those favored most by adolescent smokers.[1] We assumed, based on marketing studies, that teens were much more sensitive to advertising than adults.[2] For giving voice to these assumptions, we were called fanatics, zealots, and worse. But with the release of the documents, everything changed. With evidence like the following memo, Big Tobacco condemned itself:

> (If) we are to attract the nonsmoker or pre-smoker, there is nothing in this type of product that he would currently understand or desire. We have deliberately played down the role of nicotine, hence the nonsmoker has little or no knowledge of what satisfactions it may offer him, and no desire to try it. Instead, we somehow must convince him with wholly irrational reasons that he should try smoking, in the hope that he will for himself then discover the real "satisfactions" obtainable.[3]

The memo's author, Claude Teague, was an RJ Reynolds researcher who further observed:

> For the pre-smoker or "learner" the physical effects of smoking are largely unknown, unneeded, or actually quite unpleasant or awkward. The expected or derived psychological effects are largely responsible for influencing the pre-smoker to try smoking, and provide sufficient motivation during the "learning" period to keep the "learner" going, despite the physical unpleasantness and awkwardness of the period.[4]

Was RJ Reynolds really talking about kids in these references to presmokers? It seems so, because the "Teague Memo" goes on to say:

> Pre-smokers learn to identify with and participate in shared experiences of a group of associates. If the majority of one's closest associates smoke cigarettes, then there is strong psychological pressure, *particularly on the young person,* to identify with the group, follow the crowd . . . This provides a large incentive to begin smoking . . . Thus, a new brand *aimed at the young smoker* must somehow become the "in" brand . . . (emphasis added).[5]

RJ Reynolds wasn't the only company looking for innovative ways to hook kids. Among the once-secret documents is a memo from an October 1992 meeting of executives at Brown & Williamson, makers of Kool, Viceroy, and several generic brands, that floated the idea of tobacco-based candies, including lollipops, fruit snacks, and a "cotton-candy like product."[6] Another Brown & Williamson document states:

> In the young smoker's mind, a cigarette falls into the same category with wine, beer, shaving, wearing a bra (or purposely not wearing one), declaration of independence and striving for self-identity. Thus, an attempt to reach young smokers, starters, should be based, among others, on the following pa-

rameters: Present the cigarette as one of the few initiations into the adult world. Present the cigarette as part of the illicit pleasure category of products and activities.[7]

Brown & Williamson insisted they never approved marketing cigarettes as an "illicit pleasure" and later fired the advertising agency that proposed it. They also declared that the tobacco "candy" idea was part of a brainstorming session that was never taken seriously by anyone in authority.

One of the most ringing indictments against the industry's frequently professed "opposition" to youth tobacco use came with the release of a 1974 memo by a researcher named William Dunn, who worked for Philip Morris, maker of Marlboro cigarettes. Dunn described his company's efforts to reach kids with behavior problems:

> We wonder whether such children [who display hyperkinetic behavior] may not eventually become cigarette smokers in their teenage years as they discover the advantage of self-stimulation via nicotine. *We have already collaborated with a local school system in identifying some such children in the third grade* (emphasis added).[8]

David Goerlitz, a former Winston cigarette model, recalls asking a group of RJ Reynolds executives if any of them smoked. "Are you kidding?" one executive reportedly answered. "We reserve that right for the poor, the young, the black, and the stupid!"[9] This contempt was echoed in a 1975 proposal to Brown & Williamson by an ad agency that developed a strategy for marketing Viceroy cigarettes. Based on a series of focus groups with young people, the agency concluded: "[Smokers] have to face the fact that they are illogical, irrational, and stupid."[10]

The tobacco wars are a battle for the lives of our children. "Ask an adult when he started smoking," I once heard former FDA chief David Kessler say, "and you will hear the tale of a child." In recent years, public health efforts have focused on preventing kids from starting. Keep kids away from tobacco by passing laws that restrict youth access, the theory goes, and you solve the problem of youth smoking. Unfortunately, Big Tobacco is expert at circumventing the law. Thanks to affiliations with front groups like the National Retailers Association and the American Civil Liberties Union, laws are nothing but temporary inconveniences for Big Tobacco. And by forming ties with philanthropic organizations that offer support and silence in exchange for generous financial contributions from Big Tobacco, the industry has created an aura of innocence by association.

Many women's and minority organizations have been beneficiaries of Big Tobacco's largess. In 1992, Philip Morris gave more than $3 million to AIDS-related programs such as the Gay Man's Health Crisis.[11] The tobacco industry has also given millions for research into diseases affecting African Americans, Hispanics, and other minority populations. However, tobacco companies shy away from spending money on research for lung cancer, heart disease, or emphysema, all of which affect minority groups at higher rates than the general population. That these groups have also been targets of tobacco marketing is no coincidence, nor is the fact that they are often conspicuous by their absence when laws that would protect the health of their constituents, but negatively affect tobacco profits, are under consideration.

The tobacco industry has spread its wealth lavishly in the world of science. In addition to financing questionable studies about the health effects of smoking and secondhand smoke, it has paid scientists to manipulate nicotine levels to get consumers addicted faster and harder. During the FDA investigation into the role of nicotine in tobacco manufacturing, an anonymous donor sent the agency one tobacco company's handbook on leaf blending and product development. It described the use of ammonia to "liberate free nicotine from the blend, which is associated with increases in impact and 'satisfaction' reported by smokers." The FDA also obtained proof of Brown & Williamson's efforts to double the nicotine content of one product with something they called "Y-1," which was used as a blending tool to enable them to maintain nicotine levels while lowering tar in low-tar products. Company executives later insisted this blending tool was never used for such a purpose.[12]

One image burned into the brains of every public health advocate in the United States is the sight of tobacco industry executives raising their right hands before Congress and swearing under oath that nicotine is not addicting. In fact, the industry has long been aware of the addictive powers of nicotine, and their own documents demonstrate to what extent: "Over half [of underage users] claim they want to quit," one Brown & Williamson document states. "However, they cannot quit any easier than adults can."[13]

There has been a great deal of debate over whether tobacco should be regulated. Tobacco companies have argued that tobacco is neither a food nor a drug, and that nicotine is a naturally occurring agent in tobacco that does not fall under FDA authority. In a 1999 brainstorm, tobacco industry lawyers argued before the U.S. Supreme Court that cigarettes are "too dangerous" to be regulated. The convoluted logic behind this argument is that if the FDA applied their usual standards to tobacco, they would have to ban it. Ergo, tobacco should not be regulated, lest the 43 million Americans who currently smoke be turned into lawbreakers. The high court actually quoted this bizarre reasoning in denying the FDA authority over tobacco products. Then, in a twist worthy of Pontius Pilate, they tossed the decision back into the lap of Congress. As of this writing, it is unclear which side of the debate Congress will come down on. But if ever there was a valid argument for regulating tobacco as a drug, the notorious Claude Teague certainly pointed it out when he stated:

> In a sense, the tobacco industry may be thought of as being a specialized, highly ritualized and stylized segment of the pharmaceutical industry. Tobacco products uniquely contain and deliver nicotine, a potential drug with a variety of physiological effects.[14]

Like other drug cartels, the tobacco industry is well versed in intimidation. Everything—from sponsoring opposition to elected officials who vote against them, to using financial and legal clout to frighten journalists who investigate them, to harassing individuals who oppose them—has been employed by the industry and its affiliates such as the National Smokers Alliance. I had a taste of this when I led a group of fellow citizens in an effort to strengthen our city's clean-indoor-air laws. We'd no sooner started talking with restaurant owners and elected officials than Philip Morris gave our local restaurant association a $7,500 contribution, and letters attacking my motives and character began appearing in newspapers. I also received threatening phone calls at my home and office, though after comparing notes with advocates in other parts of the country, I realized I was a member of a large and not very exclusive club. Not long afterward, I met Jeffrey Wigand, former vice president of research and development for Brown & Williamson, who turned the tables on his ex-employer by talking to *60 Minutes* about his insider knowledge. His story, was the subject of the Academy Award–nominated film *The Insider,* starring Russell Crowe and Al Pacino. After meeting Dr. Wigand, I read the transcript of his *60 Minutes* interview and was fascinated to discover that the threatening calls he received during his trial by fire with Brown & Williamson were remarkably similar to the calls I received during our campaign in Colorado.

Years ago, when one of my Quit the Spit presenters described the tobacco industry's practices to a group of high school students, a sixteen-year-old boy raised his hand to say, "I don't believe all this stuff about the tobacco companies. If it's true, why doesn't the government do something to stop it?" This same rather naive faith is reflected in the attitudes of many smokers: "Tobacco can't be all that bad, otherwise the government would do something about it." The fact is that the tobacco industry spends more money on lobbying and campaign contributions than any industry in the world. Benefits to political candidates and elected officials include contributions to political action committees (PACs), wining and dining, hot stock tips, free tickets to plays and sporting events, and the use of corporate jets for campaign hops, political junkets, and personal vacations. And when it's time for these lawmakers to vote on matters affecting the industry, such laws have a way of disappearing in innumerable smoke-filled rooms.

If you were to check with your secretary of state, you would be stunned to learn how many local school boards and education associations are represented by lobbyists who also represent the tobacco industry. An astonishing number of hospitals, physicians and nurses associations, HMOs, and medical insurers also count as their lobbyists the same firms who represent Philip Morris, RJ Reynolds, Brown & Williamson, and Lorillard. I once worked for a health care organization that decided, for reasons I will never understand, to hire a lobbyist who also worked for the Tobacco Institute, formerly the lobbying arm of the nation's major tobacco companies. When I protested, I was informed that this lobbyist's influence with our state legislature, paid for with handsome campaign contributions, made him worth the public relations risk he represented.

One of Big Tobacco's approaches has been to hire public relations firms to convince people that the tobacco industry is neither better nor worse than any other legitimate business struggling to stay afloat in a competitive world. With all their philanthropy, the spin doctors claim, Big Tobacco deserves to be included in the community of respectable businesses. Theirs is a legal product, smoking is a matter of free will, and smokers both understand and willingly assume the risks of smoking. Leaving aside the question of conduct by an industry that has profited through unscrupulous, if not downright illegal, means, the question remains just how much free will an addict really has.

There is also a question of how much responsibility we can assign to a minor who makes what for many is an irrevocable decision. If an adult seduces a minor, the law regards it as rape *whether or not the minor is a willing participant.* Through advertising and elaborate marketing schemes, underage smokers have been seduced by the tobacco industry into making a serious, often irreversible choice before they are mature enough to appreciate the consequences. Big Tobacco itself clearly recognizes this. One more piece of the industry paper trail concedes: "Starters no longer disbelieve the dangers of smoking, but they almost universally assume these risks will not apply to themselves because they will not become addicted."[15] Another document notes: "It's fortunate for us that cigarettes are a habit they can't break."[16] By most standards of justice, this is rape.

Big Tobacco has no legitimate place in the community of respectable businesses. They are drug pushers who pay taxes. Yet as long as their smoke screen endures, the will not to believe remains strong in America's consciousness, and our outrage against injustice remains silent. Public health advocates have achieved some notable victories, including the multistate settlement and a handful of regulatory battles. But the fact remains that millions of people keep dying while millions more become enslaved, and the individuals responsible for it keep getting away with murder.

The smoker you care about is paying an unjust price for the lies and avarice peddled under the umbrella of free enterprise. That Big Tobacco can do all this and remain "respectable" says far more about our values, both as individuals and as a nation, than most of us care to think about.

Maybe it's time a few more of us did.

ꙮ Epilogue ꙮ

Years ago, when I first started facilitating stop-smoking classes, I was struck by a refrain I heard over and over again from participants: "Nobody gets it," these would-be quitters told me. "My husband/wife/parents/friends/son/daughter have no idea how hard it is to quit smoking. They just don't understand." After I went to work for the American Cancer Society, I was equally struck by calls from family and friends: "I'm worried about my husband/wife/ parents/friends/son/daughter. I've been nagging and pleading, even cajoling and threatening, but they don't seem to get it. They just don't understand!"

I believe there is a connection between this mutual lack of understanding and the high failure rates of many stop-smoking programs. No one understands. No one, including smokers themselves, realize how hard it is to quit smoking. And until some kind of understanding is forged, we are doomed to watch people we care about fail time and again to quit smoking.

An old Sioux prayer claims that you should never judge another person until you've walked a mile in his moccasins. I can empathize with smokers because I've walked their mile. I know the guilt, resentment, hostility, and alienation smokers feel when others nag, threaten, cajole, and condemn them. But as a tobacco control counselor and advocate, I also know the frustration, helplessness, disappointment, and rage of many nonsmokers. Looking back on my own years as a smoker, it hurts to recall the pain I caused my father and others who expressed concern about my smoking. I still feel guilty about smoking during my pregnancy and fear the long-term harm I may have caused my son. I shudder to think of all the friends and relatives I must have poisoned with secondhand smoke. But my repentance came only after passing through every one of Dante's circles of hell in my battle to quit smoking. And my understanding is possible only because I was able to break the power of my addict to deny that any of this was connected to reality.

I always tell people that I'm not antismoker but antismoking. My success in helping smokers quit derives from the fact that I consider them people first and smokers second. Understanding is a key component in the tobacco wars, but understanding will only arrive when we treat smokers with compassion rather than blame. Healing will only be possible when we inspire faith instead of guilt. At the same time, society must stop thinking of tobacco use as a relatively harmless, albeit annoying, habit and start treating it as the serious drug problem that it is. Society must also recognize that this is not just an individual problem but a global problem that affects everyone, whether we smoke or not.

Only when these societal perceptions shift will smoking rates go down. Only then will one-third of all cancers be eradicated. Only then will the one death in every five now caused by tobacco be replaced by people living longer, healthier, more productive lives. It won't solve all the world's problems. It won't even solve all our health problems, but it can go a long way toward preventing millions of unnecessary tragedies.

My purpose in writing this book was to allow nonsmokers to step into the moccasins of the smokers they care about. I hoped to reach smokers through those who are in the best possible position to influence and support them. In addition, I wanted to create an understanding that might build a few bridges in the bombed-out landscape of the tobacco wars. Yes, there are tobacco control warriors who lean toward fanaticism. Yes, there are legislators, insurance companies, and even health care providers who don't treat this problem with the gravity it deserves. And yet we all share a common objective: We care about our friends and family members. We want the suffering and early deaths of our loved ones to stop. We want an effective, long-term solution to the problem of tobacco use.

It's exactly what you want for the smoker you care about. Good luck and God bless you both.

☙ Resource List ❧

Below is a list of additional resources for the smoker you care about. Many of these organizations offer training, technical assistance, and literature. A few offer stop-smoking counseling or group support programs, either for a minimal charge or no charge at all. A lot of free information is also available on the Internet.

Many of the organizations listed below have chapter or unit offices scattered throughout the United States. Call, write, or e-mail them for additional information or for the address and phone number of a chapter near you.

Agency for Health Care Policy and Research
(800) 358-9295
www.ahcpr.gov
Publications on smoking cessation available for consumers

American Academy of Family Physicians
11400 Tomahawk Creek Parkway
Leawood, KS 66211-2672
(800) 274-2237
www.aafp.org
Patient materials available

American Academy of Medical Acupuncture
4929 Wilshire Boulevard
Suite 428
Los Angeles, CA 90010
(800) 521-2262
www.medicalacupuncture.org
Patient referrals

American Cancer Society
1599 Clifton Road NE
Atlanta, GA 30329
(800) 227-2345
www.cancer.org
Publications, self-help materials, and referrals; group support programs and telephone counseling are available in some locations

American College of Obstetricians and Gynecologists
409 Twelfth Street SW
P.O. Box 96920
Washington, DC 20090-6920
(202) 638-5577
www.acog.org
Patient materials available

American Heart Association
7272 Greenville Avenue
Dallas, TX 75231
(800) 242-8721
http://amhrt.org
Publications and self-help materials available

American Institute for Preventive Medicine
30445 Northwestern Highway
Suite 350
Farmington Hills, MI 48334
(800) 345-2476
www.aipm.healthy.net
Self-help materials available for smoking and smokeless (spit) tobacco

American Lung Association
1740 Broadway
New York, NY 10019
(800) 586-4872
www.lungusa.org
Publications, self-help materials, and cessation programs in some locations

Centers for Disease Control and Prevention
National Center for Chronic Disease Prevention and Health Promotion
Tobacco Information and Prevention Source
Media Campaign Resource Center
(800) 311-3435 or (770) 448-5705
www.cdc.gov/tobacco/mcrc/index.htm
Information about tobacco and quitting tips

Mayo Clinic Nicotine Dependence Center
200 First Street SW
Rochester, MN 55905
(800) 344-5984 or (507) 286-1930
www.mayo.edu/ndc
Residential (inpatient) treatment program for quitting smoking

National Cancer Institute
Cancer Information Service
P.O. Box 24128
Baltimore, MD 21227
(800) 422-6237
http://cis.nci.nih.gov
Publications available

Nicotine Anonymous World Services
419 Main Street
PMB #370
Huntington Beach, CA 92648
(415) 750-0328
www.nicotine-anonymous.org
Support groups

꧁ Notes ꧂

Part I
Introduction

1. C. Everett Koop, speech to National Press Club, Washington, D.C., 8 September 1998.

Chapter Two
Understanding Why People Smoke— And Why It's So Hard to Quit

1. Brenda C. Coleman, "Survey: Most Smokers Too Optimistic," *AP Online,* 16 March 1999. See <www.apbroadcast.com>.

2. "Tobacco Kills More Americans Each Year . . ." (New York: Smokefree Educational Services, 1993), fact sheet.

3. "Health for Life," *Newsweek* (spring/summer 1999): 13.

4. Stanton Glantz, *Tobacco Biology and Politics* (San Francisco: Health Edco, 1994), 15–20.

5. U.S. Department of Health and Human Services, *Healthy People 2000* (Washington, D.C.: GPO, 1991).

6. "Teenage Attitudes and Behavior Concerning Tobacco" (Princeton, N.J.: George H. Gallup International Institute, 1992), 54, 64, and 69, survey results.

7. U.S. Department of Health and Human Services.

8. Centers for Disease Control and Prevention, "Risky Driving Behavior among Teenagers, Gwinnet County, Georgia," *Morbidity and Mortality Weekly Report* 43 (24 September 1994): 405–09.

9. Centers for Disease Control and Prevention, *Morbidity and Mortality Weekly Report* 47 (14 August 1998): 229–33.

10. "Trend in Cigarette Smoking in the U.S.," *Journal of the American Medical Association* 251 (6 January 1989): 61–65.

11. Glantz, 8–11.

12. William Carlsen, "Heavy Smokers Blind to Risk," *San Francisco Chronicle*, 14 June 1997.

Chapter Six
Step 3: Clear the Air (Precontemplative Stage)

1. U.S. Department of Health and Human Services, "Health Consequences of Involuntary Smoking: Reports to the Surgeon General," DHHS publication no. (CDC) 8380-8387 (Atlanta: U.S. Department of Health and Human Services, 1992).

2. "Passive Smoke Is Worse for Nonsmokers," University of California at San Francisco press release, 4 April 1995.

3. Denise Grady, "Study Finds Secondhand Smoke Doubles Risk of Heart Disease," *New York Times*, 20 May 1997, sec. A1.

4. S. A. Glantz and W. Parmley, "Passive Smoking and Heart Disease," *AHA Circulation* 83(1 January 1991): 1–12.

5. American Academy of Pediatricians, *Environmental Tobacco Smoke: A Danger to Children—A Guideline for Parents*, 1992, brochure.

6. California Department of Health Services, "A Model for Change: The California Experience in Tobacco Control" (Sacramento, Calif.: California Department of Health Services, October 1998).

Chapter Nine
Step 6: Focus on the Present (Preparation Stage)

1. "Quitting Smoking Leads to Less Anxiety," *American Journal of Psychiatry* 154 (November 1997): 1589–92.

2. Centers for Disease Control, 1988 data, in "Tobacco Kills More Americans Each Year . . ." (New York: Smokefree Educational Services, 1993), fact sheet.

3. Stanton Glantz, *Tobacco Biology and Politics* (San Francisco: Health Edco, 1994), 26–27; Environmental Protection Agency, ETS Compendium,

1986 data, in "Tobacco Kills More Americans Each Year . . ." (New York: Smokefree Educational Services, 1993), fact sheet.

4. U.S. Department of Health and Human Services, Surgeon General's Report, 1985.

5. National Safety Council, 1989 data, in "Tobacco Kills More Americans Each Year . . ." (New York: Smokefree Educational Services, 1993), fact sheet.

6. National Center for Health Statistics, 1988 data, in "Tobacco Kills More Americans Each Year . . ." (New York: Smokefree Educational Services, 1993), fact sheet.

7. Centers for Disease Control.

8. Ibid.

9. National Safety Council.

10. National Center for Health Statistics.

11. Ibid.

12. Sally Squires, "Smokers Carry More Fat Around Their Abdomen," *Washington Post,* 14 May 1991.

13. Bonnie Glisson and Waun Ki Hong, "It's Never Too Late to Quit Smoking," *Journal of the National Cancer Institute* 89 (November 1997): 1782–88.

14. Centers for Disease Control and Prevention, "The Health Benefits of Smoking Cessation: A Report of the Surgeon General," DHHS publication no. (CDC) 90-8416 (Atlanta: U.S. Department of Health and Human Services, 1990).

15. Paul Recer, "Low-Tar Smokes Linked to Cancer," *AP Online,* 5 November 1997. See <www.apbroadcast.com>.

16. Denise Grady, "Genetic Damage in Young Smokers Linked to Lung Cancer," *New York Times,* 7 April 1999, sec. A15.

Chapter Ten
Step 7: Explore Stop-Smoking Treatments
(Preparation Stage)

1. Lauran Neergaard, "Smokers Can Try Anti-Smoking Pill," *AP Online,* 15 May 1997. See <www.apbroadcast.com>; "FDA Panel Backs New

Smoking Cessation Drug," Reuters European business report press release, 12 December 1996.

Chapter Eleven
Step 8: Get Physical (Preparation/Action Stage)

1. Reuters Health Information Services, "Still Smoking? Exercise May Help," 19 April 1997. See <www.reutershealth.com>.
2. "Getting Active Can Help Break Bad Habits and Form Good Ones," *Washington Post,* 23 March 1999, sec. Z20.

Chapter Twelve
Step 9: Food for Thought (Preparation/Action Stage)

1. Joseph Martorano and Carmel Reingold, *Stop Smoking, Stay Skinny* (New York: Avon Books, 1998), 7–8.
2. "Smoker's Diet Light on Nutrition," *USA Today,* 6 November 1990, sec. D1.
3. "Getting Active Can Help Break Bad Habits and Form Good Ones," *Washington Post,* 23 March 1999, sec. Z20.

Chapter Sixteen
Step 13: Consider the Link between Smoking and Depression (Maintenance Stage)

1. Reuters Health Information Services, "Smokers May Have Mental Health Problems," 12 August 1997. See <www.reutershealth.com>.
2. K. O. Fagerstrom, "Toward Better Diagnoses and More Individual Treatment of Tobacco Dependence," *British Journal of Addiction* 86 (1991): 543–47.
3. R. W. Linkins and G. W. Comstock, "Depressed Mood and Development of Cancer," *American Journal of Epidemiology* 132 (1990): 962–72.
4. Marilyn Elias, "Anti-Depressants Help Some Quit," *USA Today,* 21 April 1997.
5. Lauran Neergaard, "Smokers Can Try Anti-Smoking Pill," *AP Online,* 15 May 1997. See <www.apbroadcast.com>.

6. Neil Rosenburg, "Drug Best Agent for Quitting Smoking," *Boulder Daily Camera*, 31 May 1999, sec. 2B.

7. Harold Bloomfield and Peter McWilliams, *How to Heal Depression* (Los Angeles: Prelude Press, 1995), 37.

Chapter Eighteen
Emergency Measures

1. American Cancer Society, "Dangers of Smoking, Benefits of Quitting," public relations guide no. 2052, 1996.

2. Reuters Health Information Services, "Nicotine Patch Has Similar Maternal Fetal Effects As Smoking," 16 October 1997. See <www.reutershealth.com>.

3. "Cost Benefit/Cost Effectiveness Analysis of Smoking Cessation for Pregnant Women," *American Journal of Preventative Medicine* 6 (October 1990): 49–56.

4. J. R. DiFranza and R. A. Lew, "Effects of Maternal Cigarette Smoking on Pregnancy Complications," *Journal of Family Practice* (April 1995): 385–94.

5. Daniel A. Haney, "Study Released on Smoke, Babies," *AP Online*, 19 March 1997. See <www.apbroadcast.com>.

6. American Lung Association, annual statistical report, 1997, lung disease data.

7. Centers for Disease Control and Prevention, "Smoking Cessation Clinical Practice Guideline," AHCPR publication no. 96-0692 (Rockville, Md.: U.S. Department of Health and Human Services, April 1996), 69–70.

8. Karen Gullo, "Report: Smokers Need More Help," *The Wire: News from the AP*, 27 June 2000. See <http://wire.ap.org>.

9. Clive Bates, *Nicotine and Cocaine* (London: Action on Smoking and Health, 1999), report of a 1998 study.

10. "Smoking and Nicotine Addiction: A Pediatric Epidemic with Sequelae in Adulthood," *Current Opinion in Pediatrics* 9, no. 5 (October 1997): 470–77.

11. Centers for Disease Control and Prevention, "Recent Trends in Adolescent Smoking: Smoking Uptake Correlates and Expectations about the

Future," advance data from Vital and Health Statistics of the Centers for Disease Control and the National Center for Health Statistics, 1992.

12. Denise Grady, "Genetic Damage in Young Smokers Linked to Lung Cancer," *New York Times*, 7 April 1999, sec. A15.

13. "Cigarette Marketers' Decades Old Stereotypes May Threaten Today's Deal," *Washington Post*, 19 January 1998.

14. U.S. Department of Health and Human Services, "Preventing Tobacco Use among Young People: A Report of the Surgeon General" (Atlanta: U.S. Department of Health and Human Services, Centers for Disease Control and Prevention, National Center for Chronic Disease Prevention and Health Promotion, Office of Smoking and Health, 1994).

15. "Cigarette Smoking Key to Future Risky Behavior," Wake Forest University Baptist Medical Center press release, 15 March 1999.

Chapter Twenty-One
The Politics of Tobacco

1. Michael Siegel et al., "The Extent of Cigarette Brand and Company Switching: Results from the Adult Use-of-Tobacco Survey," *American Journal of Preventative Medicine* 12, no. 1 (1996): 14–15.

2. Richard Pollay et al., "The Last Straw? Cigarette Advertising and Realized Market Shares among Youth and Adults, 1979–1993," *Journal of Marketing* (April 1996): 1–16.

3. Claude E. Teague Jr., "Research Planning Memorandum on Some Thoughts about New Brands of Cigarettes for the Youth Market," RJ Reynolds Tobacco Company memorandum, 2 February 1973. See Campaign for Tobacco-Free Kids fact sheet (Washington, D.C., August 1996).

4. Ibid.

5. Ibid.

6. David Hanners, "Firm Says Candy Idea Merely Brainstorming," *Saint Paul (Minn.) Pioneer Press*, 23 May 1999.

7. Marie Woolf, "Tobacco Admen Think Smokers Are Stupid," *Independent* (April 1999).

8. William Dunn, Philip Morris research department memorandum, 10 June 1974, report on a company-sponsored study. See Campaign for Tobacco-Free Kids fact sheet (Washington, D.C., August 1996).

9. Bob Herbert, "Tobacco Industry Caught in Own Lies," *Denver Rocky Mountain News,* 12 February 1998, sec. A23.

10. Woolf.

11. Anna Quillen, "Good Causes, Bad Money," *New York Times,* 19 November 1992, sec. A21.

12. David Kessler et al., "Nicotine Addiction: A Pediatric Disease," *Journal of Pediatrics* 130, no. 4 (September 1997): 521.

13. Ibid.

14. Claude E. Teague Jr., RJ Reynolds Tobacco Company memorandum, 14 April 1972. See Campaign for Tobacco-Free Kids fact sheet (Washington, D.C., August 1996).

15. Federal Trade Commission, "Report to Congress for 1993, Pursuant to the Federal Cigarette Labeling and Advertising Act" (Washington, D.C.: U.S. Federal Trade Commission, 1995).

16. Maura Lerner, "Mayo Doctor Recounts Tobacco Industry's 'Smoking Guns,'" *StarTribune,* 8 October 1998.

❧ About the Author ❧

Barbara White Melin is a nationally published writer who has used her personal experience as a former smoker and professional background in communications to develop tobacco control programs and legislative initiatives for the five-state Rocky Mountain Division of the American Cancer Society. She lives in Aurora, Colorado, with her son, Eric, a college student who has never smoked.